EDUCATIONAL MANAGEMENT
Theory and Practice

J. A. OKUMBE

Nairobi University Press

First published 1998 by
Nairobi University Press
University of Nairobi
P.O. Box 30197
Nairobi

© Joshua Abong'o Okumbe

University of Nairobi Library CIP Data

Okumbe, Joshua Abong'o

    Educational management: theory and practice/J.A. Okumbe. - Nairobi: Nairobi University Press, 1998.

    275pp.; Bibl., Index.
    1. School management and organisation.
    I. Title
    LB 2805.0

ISBN 9966 846 42 5

Printed by Sunlitho Ltd., P.O. Box 13939, Nairobi, Kenya.

TABLE OF CONTENTS

	Page
Foreword	(ix)
Preface	(xi)

CHAPTER ONE
EDUCATIONAL MANAGEMENT IN PERSPECTIVE 1
Definitions and Interpretation 1
Educational Management and Educational Administration 3
The Educational Organisation 4
Organisational Effectiveness 9
School as an Industry 10
Functions of Educational Management 11

CHAPTER TWO
DEVELOPMENT OF MANAGEMENT 17
The Meaning and Functions of Work 17
Scientific (Classical) Management Movement 19
Human Relations Movement 30
Behavioural Science Movement 36

CHAPTER THREE
THEORIES OF MOTIVATION AND JOB SATISFACTION 40
Motivation and Job Satisfaction: Towards a Distinction 40
Motivation and Job Satisfaction: A Historical Perspective 42
Contet Theories of Work Motivation 43
Process Theories of Work Motivation 58
Management by Objectives 68
Goal Setting Theory in Educational Management 69
Job Characteristics Model 70
Job Satisfaction: A Contingency Approach 74

CHAPTER FOUR
LEADERSHIP, AUTHORITY AND POWER 86
Leadership 86
Authority 99
Types of authority 101
Power 102
Leadership, Authority and Power: A Clarification 110

CHAPTER FIVE
DISCIPLINE 115
Types of Discipline 116
Two Views of Discipline 117
Principles of Setting Good Disciplinary Actions 119
The Disciplinary Process 121

CHAPTER SIX
COMMUNICATION 127
Definition 127
Roles of Communication in Educational Management 128
Interpersonal Communication 129
Organisational Communication 134
The Grapevine 140
Barriers to Effective Communication 141

CHAPTER SEVEN
DECISION MAKING 145
Types of Decisions 146
Individual Decision Making 149
Participatory (Group) Decision Making 153
The Problem-Solving Process as a Cycle of Events 161
Techniques of Improving Decision Making 166
Deciding and Doing 169

CHAPTER EIGHT
SUPERVISION: GENERAL AND INSTRUCTIONAL 173
A Historical Perspective 173
Definition 175
Supervisory Activities 178
Basic Skills in Supervision 182
Supervisory Skills and Management Levels 184
Instructional Supervision In Practice: The Supervisory
Aspect of Teaching Practice 185
The Instructional Supervisor 185
The Instructional Supervision Process 186
Supervisory and Inspection 192

CHAPTER NINE
FINANCIAL MANAGEMENT IN EDUCATION 196
Cost-Benefit Analysis 197
Budgeting 197
The Planning, Programming and Budgeting Systems 204
Financial Accounting 213
Auditing 228

CHAPTER TEN
HUMAN RESOURCE DEVELOPMENT IN EDUCATION 235
The Human Resources in Educational Organisations 235
Career Development 238
Job Analysis, Job Description and Job Specification 241
Recruitment, Selection and Placement 244
Training, Development and Performance Appraisal 251
Promotions, Transfers and Separations 258
Educational Marketing 259

INDEX **265**

FOREWORD

I am gratified to write a foreword to a local pioneer work in the field of educational management. The examination of this theme is timely, coming at a time when crucial issues in education such as the cost of education, educational performance, achievement and accountability, are beginning to challenge the longstanding practice whereby educational institutions have functioned as service rather than business units, and hence the call for rigorous performance standards and management of educational institutions for effectiveness and efficiency.

It is difficult to find a single volume on the various aspects of educational management being studied at present by students of educational administration, planning and human resources development in Kenya. This book attempts to achieve this by covering a cross section of the body of knowledge, encompassing concepts, theories and practical dimensions on the process of educational management consisting of planning, procurement of resources, organising, coordinating, influencing, stimulating, integrating and evaluating in order to accomplish organisational goals and objectives. The themes have been well explicated and integrated. The orientation of ideas expressed shows a merging of theory with practice and provides pertinent information that satisfies readers' needs.

The availability of this content in one volume is indeed a most important factor in this period of scarcity of relevant locally authored books at this level.

I recommend this book to students of educational administration, planning and human resources development, to all those involved in educational management and to all educators.

PROF. FLORIDA A. KARANI
Deputy Vice-Chancellor (Academic Affairs)
University of Nairobi

August 1998

PREFACE

Educational management is not only the most fundamental and precious resource but it is also the scarcest resource in educational organisations. Indeed, most problems inherent in a number of educational organisations today do not require as many financial solutions as prudent managerial solutions. Every year millions of shillings go down the drain from the coffers of educational institutions due to poor decisioin making, problem solving, or simply lack of proper communication which often cause rumpuses, sit-ins, work restriction or simply low job satisfaction in educational organisations.

While a number of researches have been conducted and many books written in the area of educational administration and management, little effort has been expended in providing educational managers with the attendant skills in educational leadership. In addition, most publications have tended to walk a tight theoretical rope, giving readers little practice in educational management. This book attempts to present the theories and practices of educational management as an integrated subject.

The book gives a systematic, hierarchical development of educational management. Chapter One introduces the reader to the conceptualisation of educational management, its environment as well as functions. Chapters Two and Three expose the reader to both the historical development and the theories of management, while Chapter Four discusses the closely related concepts of leadership, authority and power. This is followed by a treatise on discipline in Chapter Five.

The closely related managerial functions of communication and decision making are discussed in Chapters Six and Seven respectively, whereas supervision as a management lubricant is explicated in Chapter Eight. Financial management, which is an imperative function of educational management, is discussed in Chapter Nine.

The book ends with Chapter Ten, a treatise on human resources development which derives its principles and practices from the management theories and practices discussed in the preceding chapters.

While it is difficult to come up with a book that embodies all the aspects of educational management in one treatise, effort has been expended in this book to expose the reader to as broad a coverage of educational management as possible. Further, great effort has been made to link the practice and theory of management in as precise and experiential a manner as possible so as to cater for all cadres of educational managers, students and scholars.

JOSHUA ABONG'O OKUMBE
August, 1998

EDUCATIONAL MANAGEMENT IN PERSPECTIVE

This chapter, first of all, shows the rationale for preference to use the term "Educational Management: Theory and Practice" and not "Educational Administration: Theory and Practice."

Definitions and Interpretation

The terms "management" and "administration" have been defined in various ways by many writers. It should, however, be pointed out that there are no generally accepted definitions of these terms. Infact a number of writers and practitioners have used the terms "management" and "administration" interchangeably.

The classic definition of management, however, is still held to be that of Henri Fayol. He defined management thus: "to manage is to forecast and plan, to organise, to command, to coordinate and control".[1] Brech defined management as a social process which constitutes planning, controlling, coordinating and motivating.[2] Koontz and O'Donnell defined management as an operational process initially best dissected by analysing the managerial functions. The managerial functions identified by Koontz and O'Donnell are planning, organising, staffing, directing and leading and controlling.[3] In a bid to define management, these writers have attempted to "list" what managers do.

In this book, the operating definition of management is that it is the process of designing, developing and effecting organisational objectives and resources so as to achieve the predetermined organisational goals.

The foremost task of a manager is to be able to determine the long range goals of an organisation. Having set out the goals of the organisation, the manager should be in a position to design and develop the objectives, or short range goals, and then determine both the human and material resources required for the attainment of these goals. When the objectives have been designed and put in place, the manager will then put all these entities into "effect" for the achievement of the predetermined organisational goals. Management thus performs the dual functions of policy making and executing. Management, therefore, determines both the "means" and the "ends" in an organisation.

The term administration was used by Fayol to mean management. As stated earlier, a number of writers and practitioners have used the term management and administration interchangeably. In this book, the definition of administration is that it is the process of acquiring and allocating resources for the achievement of the organisational goals. This definition presupposes that administration is a delegated aspect of management. Administration is an executive function and is therefore, a means to an end: both means and ends having been predetermined by management.

The term management has been widely used in the private sector while administration has been restricted to the public sector. This is because managers have been perceived to deal with machines and people in industries and factories where profit maximisation is the ultimate goal. On the other hand administrators have been taken to be exclusively in the public sector where work is done as a service to the society with no profit motive. The term administration has also been restricted to professional areas such as teaching, law, medicine and others where the input and output interface is not clearly defined, and the personnel are well trained in their areas of specialisation. It is thus evident that management has been restricted to the areas which do not require highly trained manpower, and where on-the-job training plays a major role in the staff development. These areas are mainly found in the profit-making organisations.

Educational Management and Educational Administration

It should be noted that educational management, or educational administration is an applied field of study and practice. It is, therefore, not a discipline on its own like, say, biology, chemistry or history. Educational management is an applied "discipline" like medicine, engineering, computer science and others, and, it therefore builds upon such basic disciplines as psychology, sociology, political science and economics. In other words, educational management refers to the application of management theory and practice to educational institutions.

The definition of educational management in this book is that it is the process of designing, developing and effecting educational objectives and resources so as to achieve the predetermined educational goals. This definition intimates that the educational manager is both a policy maker and a policy executor. Educational administration is defined as the process of acquiring and allocating resources for the achievement of predetermined educational goals. Educational administrators are, therefore, policy executors. From the foregoing definitions, it is evident that educational administration is part of educational management.

The Educational Organisation

The term organisation has been defined in many ways by different writers. Chester Barnard gave one of the earliest definitions of an organisation as "a system of consciously coordinated activities of two or more persons".[4] Etzioni, on the other hand, defines organisations as "planned units, deliberately structured for the purpose of attaining specific goals."[5]

From these definitions, it is clear that organisations consist of groups of people whose efforts are deliberately coordinated for the achievement of specific goals. An educational organisation thus refers to a group of individuals, in a given place, whose efforts are deliberately coordinated for the purpose of imparting knowledge, skills and attitudes to students or pupils in order to achieve predetermined educational objectives or goals. The "place" here refers to an institution where these efforts are unified. The educational organisations include schools, colleges, training institutions and universities. Educational organisations, like other organisations, have a number of characteristics. These are: (a) goals (b) technology (c) division of labour (d) power centres and (e) environment.

The goals of an educational organisation give it direction. These goals are derived from the overall aims of education. Organisational goals are the building blocks of the educational aims. Two types of goals must be identified and pursued by every organisation. These are: the outcome or performance goals, and the organisational maintenance goals. Educating students is a performance goal.

When schools strive to appear among the top performers in national examinations they are actually aiming at achieving their performance goal. The assumption here is that passing an examination is a surrogate measure of "being educated". The organisational maintenance goals refer to those activities which are necessary to sustain it and ensure its survival. In a school setting, such goals include maintenance of high academic and disciplinary standards, good performance in co-curricular activities, and ensuring the maintenance of an endearing public image.

Whereas the organisational goals are aimed at the achievement of the wider societal aims of education, it is important, however, that these goals be sensitive to individual teachers' goals. A teacher joins the teaching profession because he supports the aims of education in general and the goals of the educational organisation to which he is posted. However, the teacher has also got his own "personal" goals for joining the teaching profession. Such goals may include self satisfaction, earning a living and socialising in a work situation. It is important for educational managers to be aware of these personal goals since they greatly influence the manner in which teachers and other educational workers contribute to an educational organisation's goals.

The technology of an educational organisation functions at three levels: technical, managerial and institutional. The technical level refers to the activities which enable the organisation to achieve its goals. These activities culminate into teaching and learning. The function at the managerial level is to provide the technical level with an enabling environment for an efficient and effective achievement of the organisational goals. The institutional level on the other hand provides the organisation with both the legitimacy and overall direction. It also links the organisation to the outside environment. The technology of educational organisations involves bringing students, teachers and material resources together for the purpose of achieving the wider national educational objectives through a set curriculum.

However, unlike other technologies, the technology of an educational organisation is uncertain. This uncertainty is brought about by such factors as variations in teaching effectiveness among teachers, individual differences among students and the varied "environments" within which the schools are located. An example will suffice here. In a shoe manufacturing industry, the end products are shoes of given designs and patterns. Shoes of a given design are identical in all aspects. In a school setting, on the other hand, students leaving the school on completion of the final grade are varied in their educational achievements as their number.

Technology in educational organisations is complicated by the nature of the raw materials - the students - whose individual differences remain almost unaltered at the input-output interface.

An educational organisation, like all organisations, is characterised by division of labour. The labour in any educational organisation is divided among the teaching staff, non-teaching staff and, interestingly, the students who are themselves the raw materials. Due to their complex nature, the division of labour in educational organisations should be thoughtfully worked out for both efficiency and effectiveness. A sound educational management ensures proper organisation and coordination of the various sub-units within the organisation for the achievement of the overall educational aims via the organisational goals.

The power centres in an educational organisation derive their authority from acts, statutes and laws. These power centres include school committees, boards of governors, parents-teachers associations and local authorities. These power centres are charged with the responsibilities of establishing organisational goals, allocating resources and monitoring and evaluating. These power centres may delegate their authority to such lower power centres as the teachers, head teachers, principals, deans and vice-chancellors. These power centres are formal and are recognised as having authority in the organisation. However, there are also informal power centres, for instance, when groups of teachers, students and non-teaching staff assemble informally to discuss how to respond to events in an educational organisation they form an important power centre.

An educational organisation exists within an environment: it does not exist in a vacuum. The environment is divided into internal and external environments. The internal environment includes the structure, technology and people found within the organisation. The external environment refers to those organisations and forces which are found outside the educational organisation but which have an impact on its survival and effectiveness. Due to the complexity and instability of the external environment, the survival and effectiveness of an educational organisation will depend on how well it scans and adapts to its external environment.

Although educational organisations adhere to the tenets of organisations in general, they have some unique characteristics. Cohen and March have described organisations as organised anarchies[6] whose main characteristics are: unclear goals, uncertain technology and fluid participation. The specification of goals in educational organisations is difficult. If one asks the principal of a given educational organisation what the objectives of the organisation are, the answers would either be unclear or unforthcoming at all. In the same manner the identification of the technologies which will result in the implementation of the goals is an onerous task. Due to uncertainty of the goals and technology it is quite difficult to evaluate, reliably, the success of any given educational organisation. This is also compounded by the fact that non-school factors also have important influence on the achievement of the educational goals.

Another uniqueness of educational organisations is that, although they are bureaucratic, the teachers who occupy the bottom of the hierarchy are highly educated professionals. Teachers certification is very meticulously controlled by the state to ensure quality. Teachers are, therefore, supposed to be effectively involved in decisioin making in their schools due to their specialised training.

Organisational Effectiveness

Organisational effectiveness refers to the ability of an educational organisation to procure and efficiently use available resources in order to achieve the goals for which it was established. Educational organisations are established to help society achieve a number of goals which enhance acquisition of knowledge, attitudes and skills. Educational organisations may not have all the required material and human resources necessary for achievement of their goals. However, what makes an educational organisation effective is its ability to utilise its resources, even if scanty, in the most efficient manner for maximum productivity. An effective educational organisation thus provides quality education which is determined by the quality of both its input and output in the complex educational production function.

Effectiveness in an educational organisation is judged by the extent to which the organisation achieves its goals, acquires the necessary material and human resources, provides a congenial organisational climate, and meets the expectations of the society within which it is established.

The terms effectiveness and efficiency, although related, are distinct concepts. Effectiveness refers to the extent to which an educational organisation achieves its goals. Efficiency, on the other hand, refers to the cost-benefit analysis of the achievement of the goals. In efficiency, an educational manager is concerned with the least cost necessary for the attainment of maximum output from a given level of input.

School as an Industry

An education system in any country is established as a result of the determination of the broader aims of education which are in line with the aspirations of the country. To put to effect these aspirations and to ensure the attainment of educational aims, schools split the broader, long-term aims into more specific, short-term goals and objectives. To achieve this, a school implements an appropriate curriculum whose objectives ensure the attainment of aims aspired by a society. A school is, therefore, the *functional unit* of the education system. It is a processing device through which the education system meets the aspirations of the society. A school is, in economic terms, an industry which transforms a given quality of inputs into required outputs. All schools in a given society or nation can be considered as a group of industries whose functions have a summation effect on the output of the education system.

The functional role of a school as an industry is a complex one. A school is a unique industry in the sense that its raw materials, that is the students, are animate and have to be transformed into an appropriate product whose quality cannot be judged from their external appearance. The product of a school is judged by the way its past students perform in society. The education production function, which is the process by which inputs are converted into outputs, is a very complex issue. This is because non-school variables such as ability, home background and other social and economic factors also affect educational outcomes.[7]

The efficiency of a school is divided into internal and external efficiencies. The internal efficiency is determined by how a school transforms its inputs into outputs. The external efficiency of schools is judged by how well schools prepare pupils and students for their expected roles in society as predetermined by the aims of education. The efficiency of an education system, therefore, is a summation of the internal and external efficiencies of individual schools and the efficiencies of other institutions and bodies which are directly concerned with education.

In order to perform its role effectively and efficiently, a school, and by implication the education system, must be able to afford a foresighted educational leadership which is based on sound management principles and techniques.

Functions of Educational Management

The first, and foremost, function of educational management is the assurance that sound *policies, goals* and *objectives* are *formulated* in a given school and that methods are determined for the achievement of these objectives. It is incumbent upon the educational manager that he or she ensures that the policies and objectives of the school are clearly stipulated and well known to both the occupants and the society. It is through policies and objectives that the direction and destination of the school's activities can be patterned. Educational management ensures that the long-term aims of the education system are made feasible through the short-term objectives of the school.

The second function of educational management is to *procure* the *resources* necessary for the achievement of the objectives. An educational manager should be able to identify the sources of funds, the appropriate learning and teaching resources, the appropriate curriculum and above all a congenial human resource. Having identified these resources, the educational administrator then must ensure that these resources are procured in good time for the successful achievement of the objectives.

The third function of educational management is to *organise* and *coordinate* the activities of the school with the prime function of achieving the objectives of the school with maximum efficiency and effectiveness. The educational manager does the function of organising by ensuring that both the staff (teaching and non-teaching) and students are allocated duties in accordance with both their expertise and abilities. The material resources are also allocated in the most appropriate manner. It is incumbent upon the educational manager to understand the varied potentials of human resources at his or her disposal so that the division of labour is done in the most appropriate way to ensure that the objectives are achieved. In coordinating, the educational manager ensures that the varied duties allocated to individuals are unified in such a manner that all energies are expended towards a common goal. Although the various activities in the school are done in various departments or units, their sum effect is additive in that there is unity in diversity.

The fourth function of educational management is to *influence* and *stimulate* the human resources available. In influencing, the educational manager provides an appropriate organisational climate - an enabling environment - which gives the staff and students the assurance that the human factor is recognised in the school for successful achievement of the objectives. The educational manager provides articulate leadership skills which gear school's organisational structure and its personnel towards a deliberate integration of both the organisational and personal goals. In stimulating, the educational manager strives to release maximum potentials from both the staff and the students through proper application of motivation and job satisfaction theories and principles. Educational management thus recognises that human beings are endowed with abundant potentials which should be deliberately and carefully released to ensure maximum utilisation of the resources at the disposal of the school.

The fifth function of educational management is to *integrate* the school and its activities into the set-up of the society. A school is not an island - it is founded within a society for a noble role of serving the society. The educational manager does this through boards of governors, councils, parents-teachers associations, church organisations and also participation in various community activities. The idea in integration is to strengthen the school-community relations. This is important because the school derives most, if not all, of its financial and social support from the community. For the community to provide maximum support to the school, it must be seen both in words and deeds that the school is part and parcel of the society. It is thus imperative that the educational manager should effectively involve the various organisations, operating within and without, in the various and relevant school activities so as to enhance and perpetuate the school's operations. The image and prestige of a school is thus shaped through this interaction between it and the society.

The sixth, and fundamental, function of educational management is to *evaluate* the school's activities in accordance with the blueprint. Evaluation enables the school to determine whether it is achieving its predetermined objectives or not. It provides the school management with the necessary feedback for improvement, redesign or complete overhaul of the system for better results. The educational manager utilises both formative and summative evaluation techniques, and appropriate corrective, or otherwise, measures are applied and implemented as necessary. Through appropriate application of the various evaluation techniques, educational management ensures maximum efficiency and effectiveness in the school.

The above discussion looked at six functions of educational management. It must be stressed, however, that these are not the only functions of educational management. Nevertheless, these functions provide the reader with an "overall function" of educational management. It is also important to point out that the schools are set up to enable a society to achieve its objectives through teaching and learning.

Summary

This chapter begins with the definition and justification of using the term "Educational Management" where a distinction between management and administration has been provided. This is followed by the distinction between 'educational management' and 'educational administration'. The chapter then proceeds to look at the educational organisation in terms of goals, technology, division of labour, power centres and the environment. The uniqueness of the educational organisation is also discussed here. This is followed by discussions of organisational effectiveness and the school as an industry. The school, which is the functional unit of the educational system, is considered in terms of both internal and external efficiencies.

The chapter ends with the discussion of six main functions of educational management, namely, formulation of educational goals, procurement of necessary resources, organisation and coordination of activities, influencing and stimulating human resources, integrating and evaluation of school activities.

END NOTES

[1] H. Fayol, "General and industrial management," in G.A. Cole, *Management: Theory and Practice*. Essex: Spottiswood Ballantyne Ltd., 1983, p. 5.

[2] E.F.L. Brech, "The principles and practice of management", in Cole, G.A., ibid.

[3] H. Koontz and C. O'Donnell, *Management: A Systems and Contingency Analysis of Managerial Functions*, 6th edition. New York: McGraw-Hill Book Company, 1976.

[4] C. Barnard, *The Functions of the Executive*. Cambridge, Mass: Havard University Press, 1938, p. 73.

[5] A. Etzioni, *Modern Organisations*. Englewood Cliffs, New Jersey: Prentice-Hall, 1964, p. 4.

[6] M.D. Cohen and J.G. March. *Leadership and Ambiguity*. New York: McGraw-Hill, 1974.

[7] G. Psacharopoulos and M. Woodhall. *Education for Development: An Analysis of Investment Choices*. New York: Oxford University Press, 1985, p. 206.

DEVELOPMENT OF MANAGEMENT

Introduction

Management has developed or evolved as a result of man's great desire to have "things" done in the best of ways. These "things" form work which is the essence of man's existence. It is, therefore, logical that a discussion on work should precede the development of management thought. Although management was unrecognised prior to 1900, it has risen through the years to become a central activity that transcends all human endeavours. Management determines the economic progress of a country, it provides employment for the labour force, and it ensures efficient utilisation of resources.

The Meaning and Functions of Work

In the contemporary society, work has a variety of meanings. Usually people understand work as paid employment where services are exchanged for money. Work is an activity which produces something of value for other people.[1] This definition shows that work is done for a purpose and, therefore, must be productive. The definition also shows that effort expended in doing work and the corresponding wage earned must be viewed within a social context.

Work is generic, which means that the work itself is the same whether much skill or no skill is required. Some work can be interesting, rewarding and satisfying. And yet some other work can be dull, repetitive and stressful. One of the challenges of management, therefore, is to transform necessary and yet distasteful jobs into more meaningful situations which are more satisfying and rewarding for individuals and that still contribute to organisational productivity and effectiveness.[2]

The skill and knowledge of work are in the process of working and not the work itself. This point is very important in determining ways and means of making work productive. The generic nature of work implies that work can be worked on systematically, if not scientifically.[3]

For work to be integrated into the human activity of working, an indepth understanding of the work itself must be concisely undertaken. In so doing work itself will not only be made productive, but the workers will also be motivated to become achievers and get satisfied.

Work performs four main functions:

(i) Work has an economic function. Workers receive income in exchange for their labour. The money received from work is used to support the worker and his or her family.

(ii) Work has a social function in that the work environment provides the workers with an opportunity to meet new

people and make friends. Workers spend most of their waking hours with their co-workers in their work place.
(iii) Work fulfils a status function in that the type and level of one's work determine the status with which one is held in the society.
(iv) Work accords people a sense of purpose. Work determines a worker's value or contribution to society. It provides a worker with an opportunity to show his or her competence or mastery of what the work demands, and an assurance that he or she is producing something of value to both himself and the society.

Scientific (Classical) Management Movement

Although work has been central to man since time immemorial, its organised study did not begin until towards the end of the nineteenth century. Frederick Taylor (1856-1917) was the first man to have systematically studied work. Taylor is often called the father of scientific management movement. He was born in Boston, Massachusetts, in 1856. He studied in France, Germany and Italy in his youth and later earned an engineering degree. From 1878 to 1889, he was employed by the Midvale Steel Company; first as a labourer (machinist), foreman, chief draftsman and finally chief engineer. As both a labourer and manager he spent most of his time working on the problems of achieving greater efficiency on the shop-floor. He had noticed that workers were in charge of both planning and performance of their duty, a situation which according to him led to too much waste and inefficiency. In 1889 Taylor left Midvale to work in the Bethlehem Steel Company where he consolidated his ideas and conducted some of his most famous experiments in improving labour productivity. In 1911 he published his great book, *The Principles of Scientific Management*. He advocated the "man-machine," which means that man can be made to do work as systematically determined, like machines in industries.

Taylor noticed the following from his work experience:

(i) That management had no clear concept of worker management responsibilities.
(ii) That virtually no effective work standards were applied.
(iii) That no incentives were used to improve labour performance.
(iv) That systematic soldiering existed on every hand. Soldiering is the tendency to put in just more than minimal effort into daily work. There are two types of soldiering: systematic and natural. Systematic soldiering is the deliberate and organised restriction of the work rate by the employees. Natural soldiering is man's natural tendency to take things easy.
(v) That management decisions were based on intuition or rule-of-thumb or past experience.
(vi) That workers were ineptly placed at tasks for which they had little or no ability or aptitude.
(vii) That management apparently disregarded the obvious truth that excellence in performance and operation would mean a reward to both management and labour.

Taylor's Bethlehem Steel Company experiments led to the discovery of high speed steel and this revolutionised the art of cutting metals. Other experiments pertained to the way his men handled materials and tools. These were referred to as the time-and-motion-studies.

In his *Principles of Scientific Management*, Taylor advocated:

(i) *Large daily task.* Each person in the establishment, high or low, should have a clearly defined daily task laid out before him or her. The carefully circumscribed task should require a full day's effort to complete.

(ii) *Standard conditions.* The workman should be given standardised conditions and appliances to accomplish the task with certainty.

(iii) *High pay for success.* High pay should be tied to successful completion of an assigned task.

(iv) *Loss in case of failure.* Failure should be personally costly to the individual worker.

(v) *Expertise in large organisations.* As organisations become increasingly sophisticated, tasks should be made so difficult as to be accomplished by a first-rate-man.

A major criticism of Taylor's work is that it had a narrow physiological focus, and ignored the importance of psychological and sociological factors in making a worker do his or her job even better. His scientific management approach assumed that the key function of management was to have maximum production or profit at minimum cost. Efficiency was his emphasis. To realise quality and economy in production the central management was to exercise close supervision in accordance with clearly stated task performance standards.

Taylor, however, demonstrated that many jobs could be performed more efficiently even if psychological and sociological variables were completely ignored! His scientific study of work gave rise to the current techniques in job or work analysis.

Another major contributor to scientific management thought was Henri Fayol (1841-1925), a leading French industrialist. Fayol started his working life as a young mining engineer and rose to become the Managing Director of his company. In 1916 he published his famous book, *Administration Industrielle et Generale* (General and Industrial Management). Fayol's definition of management has played a key role in management literature.[4]

He stated that to manage is to forecast and plan, to organise, to command, to coordinate and to control. To forecast and plan means to study the future and arrange the plan of operation; to organise means to build up material and human organisations of the business, organising both man and materials; to command means to make the staff do their work; to coordinate means to unite and correlate all activities; and to control means to see that everything is done in accordance with the laid down rules and the instructions which have been given.

In his book, Fayol listed 14 "principles of management":

1. Division of work - develops practice and formality.
2. Authority - the right to give orders.
3. Discipline - respect.
4. Unity of command - one man one superior.
5. Unity of direction - one head, one plan for a group of activities with the same objectives.

Development of Management

6. Subordination of individual interests to the general interests.
7. Remuneration - fair for both employees and firm.
8. Centralisation - should always be there.
9. Scalar-chain: line of authority from top to bottom.
10. Order - a place for everything and everything in its place; the right man in the right place.
11. Equity - a combination of kindness and justice towards employees.
12. Stability of tenure of personnel - time for settling.
13. Initiative - all staff to be allowed to show initiative.
14. *Espirit de corps* - team work should be encouraged.

It should be noted that a major difference between Taylor and Fayol is that, whereas Taylor concentrated on increasing efficiency at the shop floor (within the operatives), Fayol was concerned with increasing efficiency among the executives (top management).

Luther Gulick and Lyndall Urwick, being strongly influenced by Fayol, put forward seven administrative functions: planning, organising, staffing, directing, coordinating, reporting and budgeting.[5] These processes are given the acronym "POSDCoRB".

Planning - working, out in broad outline, the things that need to be done and the methods for doing them to accomplish the purpose set for the enterprise.

Organising - the establishment of a formal structure of authority through which work subdivisions are arranged, defined and coordinated for defined objectives.

Staffing - the whole personnel function of bringing in and training the staff and maintaining favourable conditions of work.

Directing - the continuous task of making decisions and embodying them in specific and general orders and instructions and serving as the leader of the enterprise.

Co-ordinating - the overall important job of interrelating the various parts of the work. It ensures that all units and sub-units are working in unison towards the common objectives of the enterprise.

Reporting - the process of keeping those to whom the executive is responsible informed as to what is going on, which thus includes keeping himself and his subordinates informed through records, research and inspection.

Budgeting - concerned with all that which goes on in the enterprise in the form of fiscal planning, accounting and control.

Gullick and Urwick further put forward ten "principles." These principles were: objective, specialisation, coordination, authority, responsibility, definition, correspondence, span of control, balance and continuity.

The Gilbreths, the husband and wife team of Frank and Lilian Gilbreth, built on Taylor's ideas by developing methods of task analysis which were aimed at acquiring the best way of fulfiling a task.[6] They studied, identified and classified all the motions involved in manual work, such as "lifting", "moving", and "putting down."[7] In their *Therbligs*, which spells Gilbreths backwards, they listed a whole range of manual operations and specified how each could best be carried out, what motion it required and how much time was needed to accomplish it. In their "method study" techniques they made a considerable contribution to the understanding of work and efficiency.

Gantt, a colleague of Taylor's at the Bethlehem Steel Company was, on the other hand, concerned mainly with the payment systems. He also addressed himself to the configuration of operations in work.[8] In his Gantt charts, he starts out with the desired end product and then outlines every step needed to attain it and the time required to accomplish the task. The Gantt charts are widely used in organisations.

Another contributor to scientific management movement was Max Weber (1864-1920), a German academician and social scientist. Unlike Fayol, Taylor and others, Weber was not a practising manager. Weber's main interest in organisations was from the point of view of man's authority structure and so he wanted to find out why people in organisations obeyed those in authority over them.

His published studies were first translated from the original German in 1947. It was in the publication *The Theory of Social and Economic Organisation* that he gave the term "bureaucracy". He saw bureaucracy as a form of organisation which exists to a greater or lesser extent in practically every business and public enterprise.

A bureaucratic organisation refers to red-tape and rigid application of policies which give guidance to all the organisation's activities while almost totally ignoring the workers' needs. Bureaucracy is an organisational form with certain dominant characteristics, such as a hierarchy of authority and a system of rules. Its red tape, that is excess paper work and rigid rules, leads to inefficiency. As Hanson rightly points out, the popular usage of the term bureacracy is often associated with organisations in which top managers firmly and decisively say nothing at all, middle managers practise dynamic inaction and creative status, and subordinates specialise in cutting red tape lengthwise.[9]

Weber ascribed the term bureaucracy to the rational-legal authority whereby acceptance arises out of office, or position, of the person in authority as bounded by the rules and procedures of the organisation. The Weberian bureaucracy was admittedly a *mechanistic structure* as opposed to an *organic structure*. An *organic structure* or an *adhocracy* is flexible, adaptive and responsive to the needs of the workers.

Weber identified five main features of a bureaucratic organisation:

(i) A hierarchical arrangement of offices whereby one level of jobs is subject to control by the next higher level. Authority is thus distributed in a pyramidal manner.

(ii) Division of labour whereby tasks are divided into areas of speciality and employees are assigned tasks in accordance with their training, skill and experience in order to enhance efficiency.

(iii) Strict adherence to rules and regulations. All the organisational functions are strictly guided by stipulated rules so as to ensure conformity and uniformity among all the employees.

(iv) Impersonality of interpersonal relations. This is to say that official positions exist in their own right and the job holders have no right to a particular position. The personal, emotional and irrational inclinations must be eliminated from the organisation at all costs.

(v) Appointment to offices must be based on expertise and technical competence if work is to be performed efficiently and effectively.

In Weber's analysis of organisations he identified three basic types of authority. These are the *traditional authority* where acceptance of those in authority arises from tradition and creation as in the case of kings; *charismatic authority* where acceptance arises from loyalty to and confidence in the personal qualities of the ruler; and the *legal-rational authority* where acceptance arises out of office, or position of the person in authority as bounded by the rules and procedures of the organisation. The underlying precept of the Weberian bureaucracy was that workers were unpredictable, lazy and had no organised approach to work which increased their inefficiency at work.

Although classical management has been greatly criticised for its dehumanising approach to management in general, it has, however, been greatly applied in almost all spheres of management. If, for instance, you asked any manager how his or her organisation is generally administered, the response will mostly be in terms of, for instance, hierarchy, goals, job descriptions and lines of authority.

Scientific management advocates the establishment of goals and objectives. Education in general and educational management in particular are highly goal-oriented. It is the goals of education which the educational managers are committed to achieving in the most effective and efficient manner. The lesson plans and schemes of work have well-defined and carefully stated objectives which the teachers and the students strive to achieve. The idea of knowledge of aims, goals and objectives and duties is very important for both teachers and educational managers because productivity in education would increase if tasks are well defined. This facilitates accountability and is an important basis upon which an effective work appraisal can be undertaken.

The establishment of division of labour is advocated by scientific management. In schools, colleges and other educational organisations, departments have been created to ensure that each member of the organisation has an important role to play as an input into the overall performance of tasks as spelt out by the objectives. The division of labour in schools takes into account the principle of span of control which refers to the optimum number of subordinates under the direction of one superior. This is seen in the size of schools, size of classes, size of departments and the way the management hierarchy is developed in schools. The adherence to the chain of command is made appropriate through departmentalisation and development of a hierarchy which spells out the levels of control such as principals, deputy principals and heads of departments

Scientific management strongly advocates the scientific measurement of tasks and levels of performance. In educational management students are thoroughly tested through the use of carefully planned tests. The tests are also carefully marked with the help of carefully prepared and moderated marking schemes. Students are carefully classified by levels of performance and final certificates are awarded in line with this.

The preparation of lesson plans and schemes of work is a clear indication of the scientific management of tasks to be performed in a school within a given period of time. Scientific management also advocates the determination of the best way to perform a task. Educationists and educational scholars are continually searching for the best and most effective ways of pedagogy.

According to scientific management, the definition of rules of behaviour and the establishment of discipline among the employees are imperative. In educational management teachers' code of regulations, terms of service and school rules are well stipulated and defiant behaviour is dealt with in accordance with the laid down disciplinary procedures.

Scientific management advocates recruitment based on ability, technical knowledge and expertise. The qualifications and certifications of teachers are carefully monitored and controlled by the state. The fact that teacher training is effectively controlled by the state ensures that teachers employed at various levels are capable and technically competent to handle the various commitments of their jobs.

The scientific (classical) management movement or human engineers emphasised formal bureaucratic organisations. It was concerned with the way work was divided among workers, how power was allocated and the job specifications for each position. A glaring shortcoming of this movement is that its proponents seriously neglected individual idiosyncracies of people at work. In the machine model of scientific management, the assumption is that an organisation can be constructed according to a blueprint, like a construction engineer would build a house according to the specifications of an architect in a plan. This is a rigid conception of organisations.

Scientific management movement had a mechanistic view of organisations. It stressed form and structure of organisations and minimised human relations, disregarded psychological factors behind human productivity and further ignored the role of informal group relations on operations within an organisation. The underlying tenet of the scientific management movement was the belief that man was basically unpredictable, lazy, more emotional than rational, disorganised in his approach to problems, and that such dispositions could interfere with achieving maximum efficiency.[10]

Human Relations Movement

Human relations movement developed as a reaction against the formal tradition of the classical models. Whereas classical theorists were principally concerned with the structure and mechanics of organisation, the human relations theorists were concerned with the human factor in organisations. In other words, the human relations movement stressed organic structures as opposed to mechanistic structures stressed by the classical movement. Unlike the classical theorists who were mainly practising managers, the human relations theorists were academicians.

At the forefront of the human relations movement was Mary Parker Follett (1868-1933). She was born in Boston, later becoming a lawyer, philosopher and a political scientist. She believed that the fundamental problem in all organisations was in developing and maintaining dynamic and harmonious relationships.[11] Follett strongly maintained that conflicts were useful in organisations because they were important manifestations of socially valuable differences which were beneficial to all in an organisation.

Although Follett is credited with having pioneered the human relations movement, it was not until the analysis of the Hawthorne Studies of the Western Electric Company in Chicago that a breakthrough in this school of thought was achieved.[12] Few experiements, particularly those that focus on small groups, have been quoted or referred to more often in the literature on management than the Hawthorne Studies which took place between the late 1920s and early 1930s.[13] Research activities which were conducted during World War I had focused on ways to increase productivity by measuring the impact of physiological fatigue or other physical factors in the work environment.

The Western Electric Company, which prided itself on its welfare facilities, started conducting a number of studies into the effects of lighting on production and morale. In the first of the three early experiments, illumination intensity in each of the three departments was increased at defined intervals. The results were puzzling: the production rates in each of the three departments did not correspond with illumination intensity, nor did low illumination reduce production. In the second experiment, a test group in which illumination intensities were varied was compared to a control group with illumination held constant. The result, that both groups showed increases in production rates which were quite high, was even more puzzling. In the third, and last, experiment in this series the lighting for the test groups was decreased and that for the control group was kept constant. Another puzzling result: the efficiency of both test and control groups increased.

The Western Electric Studies also researched into how the use of incentives to work could be combined with improved work conditions. This search for the most efficient and productive work arrangements began with the now famous six girls in the relay assembly room.[14] In the relay assembly room the girls assembled electrical relays in a room specially set aside for this. In this room they were observed by the researchers. The "strange" result was that the output of the six girls continued to rise over the two years of the study despite the variations in the provision of a number of variables, such as work space and illumination, which were thought to affect productivity. Indeed these anomalous results had their explanation in psychological rather than physiological factors operating within the work environment. The researchers thus concluded that the six girls received special recognition due to their knowledge of the fact that they were the "selected few", a special group for the experiment. This is what is referred to as the "Hawthorne effect" This led to the "discovery" of an informal group whose morale and productivity increased due to their "special" treatment in the company.

The executives of the Western Electric Company solicited for the services of Professor Elton Mayo, an industrial psychologist, and Professor Fritz Roethlisberger, a social psychologist, both of Havard University so as to enable the company to understand the "strange" results from the preceding experiments. Professor Mayo (1880-1949) was an Australian by birth, a psychologist by training and a natural PR (public relations) man by inclination. In this research project the researchers measured the influence of rest pauses, lunch breaks, and length of the work-day and work-week. These experiments which were carried out for five years between 1927 and 1932 were conducted in the bank wiring observation room, where wires were attached and soldered in rows or banks to a telephone switchboard component in the work environment. In this experiment the physical conditions of work such as noise, light and amount of space were varied. The major experimental variable in the environment was a series of wage incentives. The management assumed that the employees would work harder if they were given extra pay. However, the management failed to recognise the fact that in the early years of great depression workers were more concerned about keeping their jobs by maintaining production at "safe levels" in spite of various incentives offered by management.

The puzzling results from these further experiments made the researchers to conclude that wage incentives and physical working conditions alone do not explain the level of production in an organisation. The results showed that the development of social groups with their own codes of behaviour was very important in the functioning of an organisation.[15] From these studies it became clear that when people are in continuous contact, as in a work place, they tend to form informal groups arising from their social needs.[16] The studies brought to light the importance of the social factor which is the degree to which work performance depends not on an individual alone, but on the network of social relationships within which he or she operates.[17] A number of studies, carried out on organisations have shown that informal groups which are omnipresent in all organisations greatly influence motivation to work, the level of output and the quality of work done.

The human relations movement is credited with changing the organisational style of administrators to place less emphasis on the rigid interpretation of efficiency suggested by F.W. Taylor but greater attention on obtaining cooperation of employees and helping them identify more closely with the organisation and its goals.[18] The results of the Hawthorne Studies further show that managers should not only be sensitive to people but should develop human relations or social skills for working with and through people in their organisations. Human relations movement replaced concentration on the structure of the organisation with an emphasis on employee motivation and job satisfaction. The most interesting thing about the Hawthorne Studies is that the researchers were looking for something which was different from what they found!

The Hawthorne Studies were, by modern standards of social research, relatively unsophisticated in their methodology. However, these studies provided an important milestone in the study of people in organisations.

It is important for educational managers to understand and appreciate the existence of social systems, both formal and informal, in an educational environment. By recognising and integrating these groups into the overall operations of the school, the groups would work towards the goals of the school rather than antagonise the system.

The human relations theory enables educational managers to recognise the human factor in educational organisations. Employees and students have a number of personal needs and varied talents which must be recognised and incorporated in the organisational structure. The recognition of the potentials of individual teachers, students and other workers in an organisation not only motivates them to exploit their capabilities but also sensitises them to use the available resources to upgrade their skills. All members of an organisation should be recognised both as individuals and as groups.

Individuals are endowed with a lot of talents and capabilities which educational managers should be able to detect and exploit for the betterment of their organisations. In order to detect individual talents, the educational managers should provide an enabling environment which assures the teachers, students and other workers that their ideas and contributions are important for the overall organisational efficiency and effectiveness.

Educational managers should show a noticeable concern about the conditions of the work and learning environment for teachers, students and other workers. In order to enhance the motivation of members, educational managers should exhibit a deliberate effort to improve the conditions within the work environment.

Behavioural Science Movement

The behavioural science movement is an outgrowth of human relations studies. The Hawthorne Studies stimulated social researchers and practising managers to start seeing workers in a more complex and an integrated manner. It became more apparent that the human relations movement represented an incomplete view of human behaviour in a work organisation. The behavioural science movement views workers' motivation in terms of such factors as: work itself, the nature of the incentive system, interpersonal relations, management style, workers' needs and values, and the work environment.

Behavioural science movement is an integrated approach to management which derives its theories from such disciplines as anthropology, sociology and psychology. The behavioural science research has enabled management scholars and practitioners to understand that the way people behave in organisations cannot be explained by human interactions alone, but also by such factors as organisational structure, job design, technology and management style.

Behavioural science movement assumes that different employees want different rewards from their jobs, that many employees are sincerely willing to contribute, and that employees by and large have the capacity to exercise a great deal of self direction and self control at work. It is thus the management's task to ensure that the overt and covert human potentials are exploited for the benefit of the individual and the organisation.

The next chapter provides a comprehensive treatise on some of the proponents of the behavioural science movement.

Summary

This chapter begins with an introduction, and the meaning and functions of work. Both the generic nature and the four main functions of work are elaborated. This is followed by analysis of the classical (scientific) management movement where a number of proponents of the classical management thought are discussed, as well as the application of this school of thought in educational management. Max Webers bureaucracy is elaborated here. A critique of the scientific management movement is also provided.

The human relations movement is discussed after the scientific management movement. The Hawthorne Studies as well as the Hawthorne "effect" are discussed in detail. The last part of the chapter provides a discussion of the behavioural science movement.

This chapter thus deals with work rationalisation by the classical management movement, work humanisation by the human relations movement and, finally, the integrated approach to work. In other words, the chapter shows how diametrically opposed the scientific and human relations schools of thought were, that is, whereas human problems stood in the way of production and so should be completely eliminated according to the classical management movement, the human relations movement, on the other hand, considered human problems as both a field of interest and study for the enhancement of effective management. The behavioural science movement provided the solution by integrating the scientific and human relations theories into a comprehensive management theory.

END NOTES

[1] R.M. Steers, *Introduction to Organisational Behaviour*, 4th Ed. New York: Harper Collins Publishers, Inc. 1991, p. 5.

[2] Ibid.

[3] P.F. Drucker, *Management, Tasks and Responsibilities*. London: Heinemann, 1974, p. 99.

[4] E.M. Hanson, *Educational Administration and Organisational Behaviour*. Boston: Allyn and Bacon, Inc. 1979, p. 27

[5] H.K. Hoy and C.G. Miskel. *Educational Administration: Theory, Research and Practice*. New York: Random House, 1978, p. 5.

[6] J.A. Okumbe, "Levels of Job Satisfaction Among Graduate Teachers in Secondary Schools in Siaya District and Kisumu Town," Ph.D. Thesis, University of Nairobi, 1992, p. 34.

[7] A.F. Drucker, J.A. *op cit.*, p. 200.

[8] Ibid.

[9] E.M. Hanson, *op. cit.* p. 21.

[10] S.J. Knezevich, *Administration of Public Education*, 3rd Edition. New York: Harper and Row Publishers, 1975, p. 76.

[11] W.K. Hoy and C.G. Miskel. *Educational Administration: Theory and Practice*. New York: Random House, 1978, p. 7.

[12] J.A Okumbe,. *op. cit., p. 35.*

[13] S.J. Knezevich, *op. cit. p. 77.*

[14] Ibid.

[15] J.C.S. Musaazi, *The Theory and Practice of Educational Administration*. London: mcmillan, 1972, pp. 35-36.

[16] J.A. Okumbe, *op cit.* p. 36.

[17] E. Schein, *Organisational Psychology*. Englewood Cliffs, New Jersey: Prentice Hall, 1972, pp. 31-38.

[18] S.J. Knezevich, *op. cit.* p. 78.

THEORIES OF MOTIVATION AND JOB SATISFACTION

Strong educational management requires a thorough knowledge and application of motivation and job satisfaction which have been widely proved to be applicable in educational setting. In this chapter a number of theories on motivation and job satisfaction are discussed.

Motivation and Job Satisfaction: Towards a Distinction

It is imperative that a distinction be made between these two closely related concepts before an in-depth discussion is undertaken on the various theories. This is because many people do not distinguish between motivation and job satisfaction.

Motivation is a process that starts with a physiological or pyschological deficiency or need that activates behaviour or a drive that is aimed at a goal or incentive.[1] Three key words emerge in this definition: needs, drive (motive) and incentive (goal). Motivation process, therefore, consists of needs (deficiencies) which set up drives (motives). The drives in turn help in acquiring incentives (goals).

Needs are best defined as deficiencies. They are created whenever there is a physiological or psychological imbalance;[2] for example, we feel thirsty (need for water) when the cells in our bodies are deprived of water. Drives or motives are evoked to alleviate needs. Drives are action-oriented and help in goal accomplishment. Drives (motives) are perceived as expressions of a person's needs and so they are personal and internal.

Incentives are found at the end of the motivation cycle. Incentives are those things that will alleviate a need and there-by reduce the drive or motive. Incentives are external to a person. They are made part of the work environment by management in order to encourage workers to perform tasks.

Job satisfaction, on the other hand, is defined as a pleasureable or positive emotional state resulting from the appraisal of one's job or job experience.[3] It refers to a set of favourable feelings with which employees view their work. Job satisfaction results from employees' perception of how well the jobs which they perform give them those things which they view as important to both themselves and the organisation.

Three important dimensions are identified in job satisfaction. The first dimension is that it is an emotional response to a job situation; in this sense, job satisfaction can only be inferred and not seen. The second dimension of job satisfaction is that it is usually determined by how well outcomes meet or exceed expectations; for instance, if teachers feel that they are working much harder than others, with similar or comparable qualifications, in other sectors of the economy but are receiving fewer rewards, they will most likely feel dissatisfied with their job. By the same token if teachers perceive their rewards as equitable then they will feel satisfied with their teaching job.[4] The third dimension is that job satisfaction represents several related attitudes. These attitudes are on important characteristics of the job like work itself, pay, promotion opportunities, supervision and co-workers.

The preceding definitions show that the basic difference between the two concepts is their relationship to behaviour. Whereas motivation is a direct cause of behaviour, job satisfaction is not. In other words rewards which fulfil important needs satisfy people but do not necessarily motivate them.[5] Rewards motivate people only if their behaviour is necessary in getting the rewards.

As determinants of job satisfaction, rewards may also determine motivation, but only if rewards are made contingent upon desired behaviour. The definitions further show that the concepts of motivation and job satisfaction are both coordinate and synergistic.

Motivation and Job Satisfaction: A Historical Perspective

Although human beings have interacted with one another since the beginning of time, the art and science of trying to deal with human relationships in complex organisations is relatively new.[6] During the early days, since people's needs were not quite varied and the population was low, they tended to work in small groups which were easily managed. The actual working conditions were very poor and yet they had to work for long hours so as to survive the harsh environmental conditions. It was a question of survival of the fittest and so motivation at work and job satisfaction were unthinkable.

The advent of industrial revolution presented an important opportunity for the improvement of working conditions. The industries created more goods and also improved the workers' expertise. Thus workers earned higher wages and their hours for work were controlled. This improved their work motivation and job satisfaction. During this period, about the year 1800, Robert Owen, a young Welsh factory owner, emphasised human needs of employees, and improved the conditions of work for his employees.[7] Later, Andrew Ure around the year 1835, in his manufacturing philosophy, incorporated human factors by providing his workers with hot tea, medical treatment, ventilation apparatus and medical care. However, these ideas of Owen and Ure were accepted very slowly.

Between the end of 19th and the beginning of the 20th centuries, the faster growth of industrial revolution in the West gave rise to new factories and industries and, therefore, labour was plentiful. The main problem that arose was how to combine people and machine to achieve greater efficiency for profit maximisation.

Content Theories of Work Motivation

The content theories of work motivation aim at determining what motivates people at work. These theories are concerned with identifying the needs and drives that people have and how these needs and drives are prioritised. These theories are mainly concerned with the kinds of incentives and goals which people aim at attaining in order to be satisfied so as to improve their performance at work. The scientific management school thought that money was the only incentive and, therefore, the worker was looked at as a rational, economic man. Human relations movement on the other hand felt that the incentives should include better working conditions which take into account overall individual needs.

The theories of work motivation and job satisfaction have married the ideas of scientific management and human relations movements. Five main theories are discussed under the content (acognitive) models. These are the needs-hierarchy, the two-factor, ERG, McGregor's and McClelland's theories.

Needs-hierarchy theory

Although several theorists have proposed theories which have needs arranged in a hierarchy, Maslow's work has been the most influential.[8] Maslow's studies in human motivation led him to propose a theory of needs based on a hierarchical model with basic needs at the bottom and higher needs at the top. These are physiological needs, safety needs, (basic needs), love needs, esteem needs and self-actualisation needs (secondary or higher needs). Figure 1 shows Maslow's hierarchy of needs.

Fig. 1 Maslow's hierarchy of needs

The physiological needs are the most basic in the hierarchy. They are the basic biological functions of the human organism. These needs are unlearned. Examples are hunger, thirst, sleep and sex. The safety (security) needs occupy the second level. These needs include both emotional and physical needs. Security needs relate to the desire for a peaceful, smoothly run and stable environments. Workers want some assurance that their security needs will be met. Security in a work environment ensures that workers' needs will be met now and in the future. These basic or lower-order needs are usually fairly satisfied in a work environment and, therefore, they rarely dominate.

The third level of needs is variously referred to as love, belonging, affection, affiliation or social needs. These needs are concerned with affectionate relations with other people and status within a group. Since workers spend most of their waking hours in their working environments most of the love needs should be satisfied here.

The fourth level of needs is the esteem needs. These are the needs for power, achievement, competence, recognition and status. Here, an individual aspires for self-respect, self-esteem and esteem of others. At this level individuals want to feel that they are worthy, that others also recognise this and that the individuals likewise recognise that others are worthy.

The fifth level of needs is the self-actualisation needs. At this level, one becomes what one is capable of becoming. In other words, what one can be, one must be. An individual's need to self-actualise is the need to be what one wants to be to achieve fulfilment of one's life goals, and to realise the potential of one's personality.[9] Self-actualisation influences nearly all cadre of workers. Workers choose occupations that they like, and they get certain satisfactions from accomplishing their tasks. These last three levels of needs: love, esteem and self-actualisation, are referred to as secondary or higher-order needs.

According to Maslow a person will be concerned with self-actualisation needs only if his physiological, security, love and esteem needs are well satisfied. Maslow implies that needs are arranged like a ladder that must be climbed one rung at a time. A need which has been satisfied is no longer motivating. However, if the satisfaction of a lower-order need is threatened, that need will, again, become prepotent and the efforts to satisfy all higher order needs will be reduced. The needs-hierarchy theory shows that individuals are wanting creatures with needs providing the impetus in human behaviour. It also shows that needs are universally arranged in a hierarchy of prepotency. This means that as relative gratification of a given need occurs, it submerges and it activates the next higher need in the hierarchy. It would be expected, therefore, that the kinds of things which will motivate a person may change as his or her career in an organisation progresses and as he moves up the need hierarchy ladder.

Although Maslow's needs-hierarchy paradigm has been widely accepted, there is little research evidence to support it; the five levels of needs have not been verified empirically. There is mixed support for the idea of prepotency.[10]

One of the reasons why it has been difficult to verify Maslow's theory through research is that the concepts used are vague and general. The concepts like esteem and self-actualisation have multiple definitions because an explicit definition has become elusive over the years. It has been argued that self-actualisation may not be a need at all but a socially desirable response resulting from certain cultural values.

The research instruments designed to verify this theory have serious weaknesses, for instance the popular needs satisfaction questionnaire (NSQ) does not accurately reflect Maslow's hierarchy of needs. It is also argued that Maslow's needs paradigm is a philosophical framework to describe typical attitudes of United States workers. Due to all these criticisms the needs-hierarchy theory does not warrant the unquestioning acceptance it has attained in organisational psychology and management literature.[11]

Despite growing criticisms that this theory lacks enough research support, it continues to enjoy wide acceptance in educational research and practice. This is because it presents some tangible ideas for helping organisations to motivate their workers.

Porter has carried out the longest research based on Maslow's theory. In this research which he carried out between 1961 and 1963, he modified the hierarchy of needs to include autonomy needs. He placed the autonomy needs between esteem and self-actualisation. He then developed the needs satisfaction questionnaire (NSQ). In his research he found out that self-actualisation was the most critical among managers. He also found that esteem, security and autonomy needs were more often satisfied in middle rather than in bottom management positions.[12]

Trusty and Sergiovanni adapted the NSQ for the school setting. They found that the largest deficiencies for professional educators were esteem, autonomy and self-actualisation needs.[13] They also found that administrators, when compared to teachers, had fewer deficiencies of esteem needs and more of self-actualisation needs. Their conclusion was that the lack of self-esteem received from school positions represented the largest source of needs deficiency for teachers.

In educational setting, Maslow's need hierarchy implies that educational management has a responsibility to create a work climate in which teachers and other educationists can satisfy their needs. Most primary school teachers have not met their basic needs and therefore, educational managers at this level should concentrate on the satisfaction of these needs. However, in secondary schools and higher educational institutions most teachers have met their basic needs, and, therefore, educational managers should focus on creating a work environment which satisfies the growth or higher order needs. For example, the enabling work environment should provide opportunities for greater variety in teaching methodologies, autonomy in work schedules and increased responsibility so that the maximum potentials of the teachers can be released. If an enabling environment is not provided for teachers they will have increased frustration, lower performance and job satisfaction, increased work restriction, tardiness and high turnover.

Two-factor theory

Fredrick Herzberg extended the work of Maslow and developed a specific content theory of work motivation. This theory also referred to as Herzberg's two-factor theory, motivation-hygiene theory or dual-factor theory, is based on the assumption that dissatisfaction leading to the avoidance of work and satisfaction leading to attraction of work do not represent the end points of a single continuum.[14] Instead, two separate unipolar continua are required to reflect people's dual orientation to work; hence the two-factor theory. The independence of these two scales results from two distinctive sets of job factors that apply to only one of the continua.

Herzberg conducted a motivational study on 200 accountants and engineers employed by firms in and around Pittsburgh, Pennsylvania. He used the critical incident method of obtaining data for analysis. Each employee was asked to recall an event or a time personally experienced at work when he felt particularly and exceptionally good about his job. Further interviews were conducted to find out why the employees felt as they did, and whether their feelings of satisfaction had affected their performance, their personal relationships, and their feelings of well-being. These respondents were also asked to recall an event or a time personally experienced at work when they felt particularly and exceptionally bad about their jobs. Further interviews were conducted to find out the nature of the events which led to the negative expressions.

These responses were content analysed and the following conclusions were derived:

(1) Factors which are associated with the job-itself (intrinsic, job-content or psychological factors) tend to lead to job satisfaction. These factors include achievement, recognition, work itself, responsibility and advancement.

(2) Factors which are associated with the environment surrounding the job (extrinsic, job-context, physical, environmental or maintenance factors) do not tend to lead to job satisfaction. These factors include company policy and administration, supervision, salary, interpersonal relations and working conditions.

(3) Job satisfiers are generally determiners of long-term changes, and job dissatisfiers are generally determiners of short-term positive changes of attitudes.

(4) Job satisfiers are called motivators because they fulfil an individual's need for psychological growth. Job dissatisfiers are called hygienes because they merely serve to prevent an individual from "feeling bad" about work.

Herzberg's theory is closely related to Maslow's need hierarchy. The hygiene factors are roughly equivalent to Maslow's lower-order needs. According to Herzberg, the hygiene factors prevent dissatisfaction, but they do not lead to satisfaction. In other words, they bring motivation to a theoretical zero and, therefore, prevent dissatisfaction. The motivators are equivalent to Maslow's higher-order needs. It is only the motivators which motivate workers on their job. This theory indicates that a worker must have a job with a challenging content in order to be truly motivated. In other words, work satisfaction and dissatisfaction are not opposites rather they are separate and distinct dimensions of work orientation.

Herzberg's two-factor theory has been one of the most researched in organisational behaviour and, therefore, it has been the target of severe criticism. The most devastating criticism, however, has been that the theory is method bound. The results, which were produced by Herzberg and his associates in 1959 can only be replicated when the critical-incidents technique is used. King concluded that most studies using the Herzberg technique support the motivation-hygiene theory, but most studies using a different method do not.[15] It has also been found that there are job factors that lead to both satisfaction and dissatisfaction.

Although the two-factor theory has obvious limitations, Herzberg is greatly credited with his substantial contribution to the study of work motivation. He not only extended the Maslow's needs-hierarchy but was also instrumental in the "discovery" of job enrichment, a technique widely used in job design. In spite of the fact that the two-factor theory lacks a comprehensive theory of work motivation and does not adequately describe the complex motivational process of organisational participants, it has however, contributed immensely to the better understanding of job content and job context factors and satisfaction. Steers and Porter believe that Herzberg's ideas filled a void in the late 1950s by calling attention to the need for improved understanding of the roles played by motivation in work organisations.[16]

Herzberg's findings have implications on educational management. The teachers' motivation can be improved through changes in the nature of the job through job enrichment. Teachers should be enabled by the management to have maximum control over the mechanisms of the task performance, and their jobs should be so designed as to enable them to experience a feeling of accomplishment of assigned tasks. Educational managers should ensure that teachers are provided with direct, clear and regular feedback on their performance in particular and the organisational performance in general. It is also imperative that teachers should be provided with an enabling environment, by the management, so as to motivate them to learn new and different procedures on the job and also experience some degree of personal growth through promotion and further training.

ERG theory

Glayton P. Alderfer modified Maslow's original theory. This was because of the failure of Maslow's needs-hierarchy to hold up to empirical validation. Alderfer formulated Maslow's five needs-hierarchy into three more general need levels and identified three groups of core needs: existence needs, relatedness needs and growth needs, hence the ERG theory. The existence needs are concerned with sustaining human existence, including physiological and safety needs. The relatedness needs are concerned with how people relate to their surrounding social environment. This includes the need for meaningful social and interpersonal relationships. The growth needs relate to the development of human potential which includes self-esteem and self actualisation. The growth needs are the higher level needs.

Alderfer's needs-model is similar to Maslow's needs-hierarchy in a number of respects. However, the two models differ on two important aspects. The first difference is that, whereas according to Maslow, workers move up the hierarchy when the lower need has been fully satisfied and the next need becomes prepotent, Alderfer's ERG theory on the other hand suggests that there is also a frustration-regression process in addition to the satisfaction-progression process. This is to say that when a teacher is continually frustrated in his or her attempts to satisfy growth needs, the relatedness needs will re-emerge as a strong motivating force thus the efforts are re-directed towards the lower-order needs. A second difference is that the Alderfer's theory suggests that more than one need may be operating at the same time, unlike Maslow's prepotency rule. Alderfer's ERG theory is less rigid than Maslow's needs-hierarchy and allows for greater flexibility in describing human behaviour.[17]

Although there has not been much research on the ERG theory, most contemporary analyses of work motivation tend to support this theory over Maslow's and Herzberg's.[18]

McGregor's theory X and theory Y

Douglas McGregor's Theory X and Theory Y are mainly sets of assumptions about behaviour of people at work.

Theory X refers to a set of assumptions about employees, namely:

- that they are lazy;
- that they dislike work and will avoid it;
- that since they dislike work they must be coerced inorder to do it;
- that they will avoid responsibilities and so will seek to be led; and
- that most employees are self-centred in that they place security above all other factors.

So the only way that management can make employees to achieve high performance is to coerce, control and even threaten them. Theory X emphasises strict employee control and the application of extrinsic rewards.

Theory Y employs a humane and supportive approach to management. It assumes that employees:

- are not inherently lazy;
- view work as being as natural as rest or play;
- will exercise self direction and self control if they are committed to the objectives;
- can, on average learn to accept, even seek responsibility; and
- that the ability to make innovative decisions is widely dispersed throughout the population.

According to this theory, the manager's role is that of providing an enabling environment for the release of potentials which employees are endowed with.

McGregor's theory X and theory Y have made a commendable impact in the management world and will be seen in leadership styles (Chapter 4) and discipline (Chapter 5). The theory X and theory Y assumptions about employees help educational managers to identify extreme forms of management styles which can be blended for effective management.

McClelland's achievement motivation

Extensive research on achievement motivation was done by David C. McClelland of Havard University.[19] McClelland's studies showed that people's motivation patterns reflect their cultural environment including family, the school, the church and the work place. McClelland and his research team studied the three basic needs namely; need for achievement (n-Ach), need for power (n-Pow) and need for affiliation or belonging (n-Aff).

Need for achievement. The need for achievement or achievement motivation is a drive that some workers have in order to overcome the challenges and obstacles which they encounter in the process of goal attainment. Employees with high need for achievement have the following characteristics:

(i) A tendency to set moderately difficult goals. The high achievers like to set their own goals which they thoughtfully select and become committed to. They like to be as fully responsible for the attainment of their goals as possible; they would rather accomplish a task successfully than leave it to chance.

(ii) A desire for concrete and timely feedbacks on task performance. Since high achievers attach great importance to a goal, they would like to know how well they are doing. This is the main reason why high achievers choose challenging professional careers. They exude high self confidence and thus place a high value on their work performance. It should be noted that achievement motivation is very low when achievers are performing routine, boring, unchallenging and non-competitive tasks.

(iii) A single minded pre-occupation with task and task accomplishment. High achievers put much of their energy on a task to ensure that it is not only accomplished, but that it is also done to the best of their knowledge and capability.

Need for achievement is very important in educational organisations because the attainment of quality education requires this drive in order to be successful. Education is a highly results-oriented (achievement oriented) discipline, in the sense that prospective employees or candidates are judged by the grades on their certificates. This implies that educational managers must strive to enhance achievement motivation among teachers, students and other employees so as to provide quality education. Need for achievement has important implications for job enrichment which enhances variety, identity, significance, autonomy and feedback on the job for increased performance.

The need for achievement can be learned at an early stage, beginning at home and then in school and finally at the place of work. It is, however, estimated that only 10 per cent of the population has high need for achievement.

McClelland has provided four steps for encouraging achievement motivation among adults:[20]

(i) Teaching participants how to think, talk and act like persons with high need achievement.
(ii) Stimulating participants to set higher, but carefully planned and realistic, work goals for themselves.
(iii) Providing the participants with knowledge about themselves.
(iv) Creating team spirit among participants by encouraging them to learn about each other's successes, failures and intentions.

The needs for affiliation (n-Aff) and power (n-Pow) are not as well researched as the need for achievement (n-Ach). However, definitions will suffice here.

Need for affiliation refers to an attraction to another person or group so as to feel that one is accepted. Employees with need for affiliation have a strong desire for reassurance and approval; a tendency to conform to valued norms; and a sincere interest in the feelings of others. It has been found out that employees with high need for affiliation (n-Aff) have low absenteeism and perform better when their efforts are appreciated. Educational managers should thus create a cooperative and supportive work environment where positive feedback is consciously tied to work performance in an organisation.

Need for power (n-Pow) refers to the desire to influence others and to control one's environment. The need for power takes two forms, namely; *personal power* which refers to domination just for its sake; and *institutionalised power*, which is concerned with the attainment of organisation's goals. It should be noted that power-oriented managers, if driven by organisational effectiveness, can help in providing the impetus necessary for the facilitation of goal-oriented behaviour among their groups. Educational managers should be able to detect employees who possess need for power which is well intended for the overall organisational effectiveness. Such need for power should be enhanced for the achievement of goals in educational organisations.

Process Theories of Work Motivation

While the content or acognitive theories of work motivation are concerned with what motivates people at work, the process or cognitive theories, are mainly concerned with the preceding cognitive factors which go into motivation or effort. The process theories are concerned with the way these variables relate to one another.

Expectancy theory

The expectancy theory of work motivation was originally proposed by the pioneering psychologists Kurt Lewin and Edward Tolman as part of their *purposive psychology of behaviour* (cognitive concepts) in 1932. In 1964, the expectancy theory was formulated and aimed directly at work motivation by Victor Vroom. This theory rests on the assumptions that motivation is a conscious process in which decisions lawfully relate to psychological events that occur contemporaneously with behaviour, and that forces in the individual and environment combine to determine behaviour. Vroom explained that motivation is a product of three factors which he referred to as valence, expectancy and instrumentality.

Valence refers to the strength of a person's preference for a particular outcome such as reward. For example, if a teacher strongly wants a promotion, then promotion has a high valence for that teacher. Valence for a reward is unique to each employee, is conditioned by experience, and may vary substantially over a period of time as old needs become satisfied and new ones emerge. An outcome is positively valent when a person prefers attaining it to not attaining it. An outcome is considered to have a zero valence when a person is indifferent to attaining or not attaining it. An outcome has a negative valence when a person prefers not attaining it to attaining it.

The kind of valence that workers attach to outcomes (rewards) is influenced by such factors as age, education and the type of work; for instance, a young teacher is likely to give less emphasis to a retirement benefit than an old teacher. Likewise, a newly trained graduate teacher may have a stronger desire for career advancement than an older teacher with less education. Some employees will find intrinsic valence in the work itself particularly if they have a strong work ethic or competence motivation. These workers derive their job satisfaction directly from their work through a sense of completing their tasks effectively and efficiently. In this circumstance an employee is in full command of outcomes and he is, therefore, less subject to the extrinsic reward system of the management.

Expectancy is the probability (ranging from 0 to 1) that a particular action or effort will lead to a particular performance (first-level outcome). The specific outcomes attained by a person are dependent not only on the choices that the person makes, but also on events beyond his or her control. For instance, a teacher may not be a hundred per cent certain that the success of his or her students in an examination will be a hundred per cent since this depends on a number of factors beyond his or her control. Expectancy is thus an effort or performance probability.

Instrumentality on the other hand, is the probability (also ranging from 0 to 1) that performance (first-level outcome) will lead to a desired reward (second-level outcome). It represents the belief by the employee that a reward will be received once the task has been accomplished.

The core of the expectancy theory relates to how a person perceives the relationships between effort, performance and rewards. An example would suffice here. Promotion could be seen by a newly employed graduate teacher as an attractive prospect (valence) but his expectancy of gaining promotion could be low, if he perceives that promotion is attained primarily on length of service. In a situation like this, the teacher sees that performance does not lead to rewards immediately, so his effort in that direction is not seen as worthwhile. It should be noted, however, that effort does not necessarily lead to effective performance. For instance, an individual may have insufficient knowledge and skills or his perception of his role may be poor.

The multiplicative formulation for the relationships between valence, expectancy and instrumentality is that the force of motivation (FM) is the product of expectancy (E) and the sum of the cross products for instrumentality (I) and valence (V) items. Symbolically this is stated as:

$$FM = E\left(\sum IV\right).$$

This formula shows that the motivation of a worker to behave in a certain way changes as the level of each variable increases or decreases. Since the relationships are multiplicative, if one of the variables is zero, effort is also zero.

The three factors in the expectancy model may exist in an infinite number of combinations. The combination that produces the strongest motivation is high positive valence, high expectancy and high instrumentality. In a work situation people develop expectancy and instrumentality estimates through direct experiences and observation. The consequence of this is that employees perform some kind of cost-benefit analysis for their own behaviour at work. If the estimated benefit is worth the cost then the employees are likely to apply more effort.

One of the weaknesses of the expectancy theory is that it over-intellectualises the cognitive processes that individuals use when selecting alternative actions.[21] That people actually calculate probabilities and values, multiply them together and then decide how to act sounds too hypothetical. Another shortcoming is that the expectancy theory lacks the power to explain large percentages of variance in criterion variables such as effort and performance.

Although the expectancy theory exhibits a number of deficiencies it does, however, recognise the complexities of work motivation unlike the content theories of work motivation which oversimplify human motivation. It is evident that it does not provide specific suggestions on what motivates organisational members as the content theories, but it indicates the conceptual determinants of motivation and how they are related. The theory helps to clarify the relationship between individual and organisational goals.

The expectancy theory provides educational managers with a strong conceptual framework for understanding how motivation and performance can be improved. The teachers' beliefs that their efforts will lead to performance can be enhanced through a number of ways, such as further training, supervision, guidance, counselling and participation in job-related decisions in staff meetings. By enhancing teachers' abilities in this way they will feel that high levels of performance are feasible. Educational management should also design reward systems which are based on actual performance. The performance-reward contingencies should be increased so that teachers are assured that good work is equitably rewarded. This encourages them to work hard not only for their personal growth, but also for the successful achievement of the educational objectives.

It is incumbent upon educational managers to ensure that teachers are matched to their jobs. Educational management should be cognisant of the teachers' abilities and traits so that these are used in job placement in order to enhance performance. Educational managers should clarify job objectives during the teachers' induction or orientation. This minimises wastage of effort in search behaviour and enhances more task-related behaviour. The expectancy model provides educational managers with a strategy for integrating teachers' needs, desires and goals with those of the educational organisations.

Equity theory of work motivation

This theory has its roots from the cognitive dissonance theory and exchange theory. Earlier, it was developed by Festinger as a social comparison theory. Festinger's hypothesis was that people have a drive for evaluating their opinions and attitudes.[23] People, according to Festinger, prefer using objective criteria for comparison, but in the absence of these they compare themselves with other persons having similar ability and opinions.

Festinger's earlier work on social exchange theory was refined by Stacy Adams into what is now popularly known as the "equity theory of work motivation". According to this theory, individuals compare the ratio of their inputs and outcomes to the input-outcome ratios of another person. The theory argues that a major input into job performance and satisfaction is the degree of equity or inequity that people perceive in their work situations. Adams argues that "inequity exists for a person whenever he or she perceives that the ratio of his or her outcomes to inputs and the ratio of Other's outcomes to Other's inputs are unequal."[23]

$$\frac{\text{Person's outcome}}{\text{Person's inputs}} = \frac{\text{Other's outcome}}{\text{Other's inputs}}$$

If an inequity is seen in this equation, the individual worker will act to reduce the perceived deprivation or overpayment by either altering his inputs or outcomes, or attempting to alter the comparison person's inputs or outcomes; or he may cognitively distort any of these four factors. Examples of inputs are age, sex, education, social status, organisational position, qualifications and the workers effort or energy expended in the work. Outcome variables include rewards like status, pay, promotion (extrinsic) and interest in the job (intrinsic). Individuals always strive to restore the ratio to equity. The equity theory (or discrepancy) hypothesises a direct positive relationship between the level of job satisfaction and the perceived difference between what is expected or perceived as fair and what is actually experienced in the job situation.

When a worker's needs which motivate him or her are satisfied by the organisation's reward system then no dissonance exists and so his or her job satisfaction is high. However, when a worker's needs are greater than the rewards received for work, then a discrepancy exists which leads to dissatisfaction. On the other hand, rewards which are in excess of needs yield positive job satisfaction.

Most research testing the validity of the equity theory has been supportive. Research studies carried by Ilgen and Hamstra[25] and Hamner and Harnett[25] have shown the level of satisfaction or dissatisfaction with the outcomes received to be a function of two comparisons. In the first case a person compares his or her actual performance with his or her expected level of performance. In the second case the person compares his or her actual performance with the perceived performance of a reference person.

Hamner and Harnett found in their studies that workers who exceeded their goals were significantly more satisfied than those who failed to meet their goals. They also found that those workers whose outcomes exceeded their comparison person's outcomes were significantly more satisfied than those whose outcomes fell short of their comparison person's outcomes.

In educational setting, research carried by Miskel et al.[26] and Ortloff[27] have supported the equity theory of work motivation. Although equity theory is not a complete explanation of employees' motivation, it does describe several important motivationally relevant processes which educational managers should understand.[28] A very important implication of the equity theory in educational management is that educational managers should always be aware of the social comparison processes among the teachers themselves and also between them and those working outside the teaching profession. For instance, if teachers still think that their salaries are inequitable compared to others' with similar qualifications in the public service then there is little reason to expect them to increase their effort in their teaching assignments. Educational managers should ensure that equitability is maintained both within the teaching profession and other comparable professions.

Equity theory requires educational managers to have a thorough evaluation of the way in which the rewards are distributed among teachers. The way the rewards are distributed should in no way affect the teachers' perceptions of their own state of equity and their willingness to respond and participate.

Goal setting theory

The main proponents of this theory were Edwin A. Locke and Gary P. Latham. Goal setting theory shows how the field of organisational behaviour should progress from a sound theoretical foundation to sophisticated research and to actual application of more effective management practice.[29] It lies at the centre of performance-based motivation programmes which are effectively applied in human resources management in the form of management by objectives, (MBO).

In 1968 Edwin E. Locke presented a seminar paper which has been considered as the pioneering work on goal-setting theory. In this paper, Locke suggested that goal-setting theory can be traced back to Taylor's scientific management movement. The theoretical formulation of goal-setting theory is very similar to the expectancy theory. According to this theory, Locke indicates, the values and value judgements are important cognitive determinants of behaviour.[30] Locke defines values and value judgements as the things the individual acts upon to gain and or keep. Locke further says that emotions or desires are the way a person experiences these values. Intentions or goals, which act together with values, are also important determinants of behaviour. It is at this point where the goal-setting theory goes beyond the expectancy theory.

According to Locke, people work hard to achieve goals so as to satisfy their emotions and desires. Locke emphasises that for goal setting theory to work employees must show commitment to the goals which they set. He defines commitment as one's attachment to or determination to reach a goal, regardless of the goal's origin.[31] After an employee has set the goals to be achieved he or she then responds and performs accordingly. The results of these responses are consequences, feedback or reinforcement. Figure 2 graphically represents the steps in Locke's goal-setting theory:

Fig. 2 Locke's goal setting theory

Goal setting performs four important functions for employees. The first function is that goal setting helps an employee to focus his or her attention on a particular task or objective. The second function is that goals regulate or increase employees' efforts. The third function of goals is that they enhance workers' persistence on a task. Goals constantly remind workers of where they are moving to and how they are moving. The fourth function of goals is that they make workers become more creative in charting out new strategies and action plans for achieving the agreed upon results.

A four-step goal setting model

In Figure 3 below, a four step model for an appropriate goal-setting is outlined.

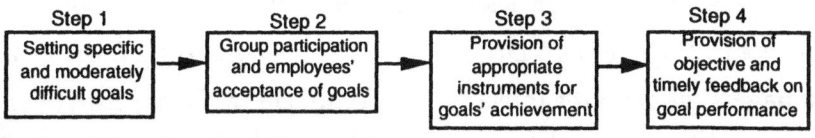

Fig. 3 A four-step goal setting model

Step 1: Managers set out specific goals which are not too difficult for workers to achieve. The goals should be measurable and challenging. Research studies have shown that difficult and achievable goals lead to better employee-performance than relatively easy goals. If the goals are too difficult to achieve, workers will feel frustrated and this reduces their motivation and hence work performance.

Step 2: In this step workers are made to participate in goal setting so that they feel that these goals are their own. Workers who effectively participate in the goal setting process perform better than those for whom goals have been prescribed.

Step 3: Management provides the workers with appropriate support, for goal-achievement. Management should ensure that an enabling environment is provided to the workers for efficiency and effectiveness in goal attainment.

Step 4: In this final step, management should provide an objective and timely feedback about the employees' progress towards goal attainment. The feedback should tell employees what they are doing right and what they are doing wrong. Feedback should be well timed if employees are expected to benefit from it.

Management by objectives (MBO)

The best known application of goal-setting is in the very popular and universally used management by objectives (MBO). MBO was first coined by Peter Drucker in the 1950s in his classic book, *The Practice of Management*. Drucker aimed at harmonising individual managers' goals with those of the organisation. Drucker felt that MBO would lead to improved organisational performance and employee satisfaction. Figure 4 shows the five steps in an MBO programme.

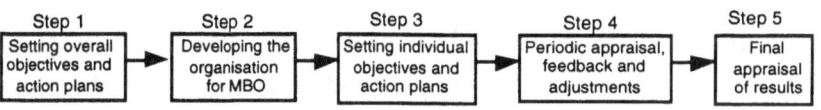

Fig. 4   An MBO model

The first MBO step involves identification of key results areas in the organisation and the determination of measures of performance. The objectives are stated and agreed upon at this stage. In the second stage the workers and the organisation are developed for effective application of MBO. In the third stage individual objectives are set and action plans determined. The individual objectives are determined by both the superior and his or her subordinate. Periodic appraisal is the fourth stage. This appraisal is diagnostic and takes place roughly every three months. The final appraisal is done once every year in the fifth stage and provides an overall diagnosis and evaluation. The MBO cycle starts again at the beginning of the following year.

Goal setting theory in educational management

Goal-setting theory is widely applied in educational management since education is a highly result oriented discipline. At the outset, educational managers must set general aims of education which are in line with the educational policies of the country.

Educational managers need to tailor the goals of educational institutions to the needs of the students and teachers. In other words an enabling environment has to be created so that the varied individual needs of the teachers and the students can be met. The educational managers have to ensure that teachers participate in goal setting and that these goals are neither too rigid nor too difficult to be achieved. Educational management should help teachers to achieve their goals through lesson plans, schemes of work and participative decisioin making in staff meetings.

Job characteristics model

The job characteristics model is considered under the process theories of motivation because it has its origins in expectancy theory. This theory was developed by J. Richard Hackman and Greg Oldham in 1976.

The job characteristics model recognises that certain job characteristics contribute to certain psychological states and that the strength of employee's need for growth has an important moderating effect.[32] In the model, five job characteristics have been identified: skill variety, task identity, task-significance, autonomy and feedback. The three critical psychological states are experienced meaningfulness of the work; experienced responsibility for work outcomes; and knowledge of results from work activities. According to Hackman and Oldham, skill variety, task identity and task significance lead to experienced meaningfulness; autonomy leads to the feeling of responsibility — the degree to which the individual feels personally accountable for the results of the work he or she performs — and feedback leads to the knowledge of results — the degree to which the individual knows and understands on a continuous basis how effectively he or she is performing the job.[33] The more these three psychological states are present, the more employees will feel good about themselves when they perform well.

The basic tenet of this model is that internal rewards are obtained by an individual when he or she learns (knowledge of results) that he or she personally (experienced responsibility) has performed well on a task that he cares about (experienced meaningfulness).[34] Figure 5 shows a job characteristics model by Hackman and Oldham.

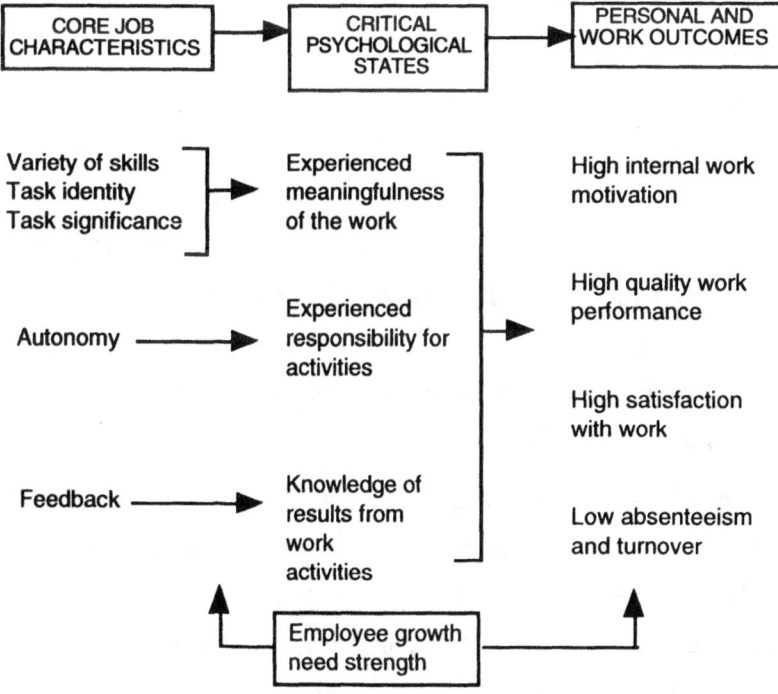

Fig. 5   The Hackman and Oldham's job characteristics model

According to this model, the motivating potential score (MPS) is the product of meaningfulness, autonomy and feedback:

$$MPS = \frac{[SV + TI + TS]}{3} \times Autonomy \times Feedback$$

where SV is skill variety
TI is task identity and
TS is task significance.

In this formula, since skill variety, task identity and task significance are additive, any one or even two of these characteristics could be completely missing and the person could still experience meaningfulness, but if either autonomy or feedback were missing, the job would offer no motivating potential score (MPS = 0) because of the multiplicative relationships.[35] This shows the major roles played by autonomy and feedback in the model. Hackman and Oldham emphasised later that the MPS of a job is not itself the cause of employees internal motivation or job satisfaction. Instead, it is jobs which are high in motivating potential which create conditions that reinforce employees who have high performance levels.

One of the shortcomings in this theory is that individual differences exist among people and how best to define, measure and include variations among individuals in the model remains open to question. The other shortcoming is that the links between job characteristics and psychological states may not be as strong as suggested by the original formula. A job-based feedback is difficult to determine and, therefore, the term feedback as is used in this model needs redefinition. Finally, the model does not clarify how an individual's perceptions relate to the objective properties of the job.

Although the job characteristics model is relatively new, a number of studies on it have been published. Hackman and Oldham developed a questionnaire, the job diagnostic survey (JDS), to analyse jobs and used this instrument in their initial field research. The research results supported the major generalisations of the theory.

In his study, Katz investigated the relationships between overall job satisfaction and five task dimensions of skill variety, task identity, task significance, autonomy and feedback from job for employees at different stages of their careers.[36] This was measured by the employees' length of employment on their current jobs as well as in their current organisations. Approximately 3500 respondents from 4 different governments — two metropolitan, one county and one state — participated in the collection of survey data. The data analysis showed that the strength of the relationships between job satisfaction and each of the task dimensions depended on both job longevity and organisational longevity of the sampled individuals. For employees new to an organisation, only task significance was related positively to job satisfaction, while autonomy had a strong negative correlation.

Whereas studies by Terburg and Davis, Kiggundu, Bhagat and Chassie and Oldham and Miller have supported the model, other studies have either indicated partial or no support.[37] Studies which fully test the applicability of this model in the educational settings have not either been conducted or documented. However,

Pastor and Erlandson using a portion of the JDS called the higher-order-need strength found that the needs of secondary school teachers are predominantly higher order in nature and that these needs are positively related to job satisfaction.[38]

Job Satisfaction: A Contingency Approach

In spite of limited research on the effect of marital status on job satisfaction, consistent research indicates that married employees have fewer absences, undergo less turnover, and are more satisfied with their job.[39] Marriage imposes increased responsibilities that may make a steady job more valuable and important.[40]

Porter and Steers have found that the older one gets, the less likely he or she is to quit the job.[41] As workers get older, they have fewer alternative job opportunities and they are also less likely to resign because their longer tenure tends to provide them with higher wage rates, longer paid vacations, and more attractive pension benefits. There is overwhelming evidence indicating a positive association between age and satisfaction, at least up to age sixty.[42]

Studies carried by Herzberg et al in 1955 showed a consistent trend in job attitudes according to age and length of service. When people begin work, they appear to do so with a considerable degree of enthusiasm. This enthusiasm soon wanes, giving way to a steady decline in job morale which reaches its lowest depths in the early thirties. It is evident from research studies that workers in the middle twenties to early thirties are the least satisfied group. When a person is employed for the first time he tends to compare his first job with his school, college or university experience since he has had no prior job experience with which to compare. The school, college or university experience is characterised by a variety of activities, acquaintances and opportunities for achievement which a newly employed worker may not find in his new job, thus causing dissatisfaction.

When young workers come to the work place for the first time, they bring with them high expectations that may not be fulfiled, as jobs prove insufficiently challenging or meaningful. When these unrealistic expectations fall short of their expectations, they endure the first decade of work with gradually increasing disillusionment. After some point in working, workers' expectations are modified and the job is seen in a more positive manner.

Sex differences in job satisfaction show less consistency. Research studies carried out up to mid 1950s showed no clear-cut differences between males and females. Research carried by Sheppard and Herrick in 1972 showed that females were less satisfied than males, the difference reaching its maximum extent among workers under thirty.[43] It appears from these findings that women, especially young women, are less likely to be satisfied with just any form of employment; they are quite understandably more sensitive about working under job conditions which are inferior to those prevailing among males with the same set of qualifications as their own.

Employees tend to prefer work which is mentally challenging. They prefer jobs which give them opportunities to use their skills and abilities and offer a variety of tasks, freedom and feedback on how well they are doing. A job becomes more challenging if it has these characteristics and this increases workers' job satisfaction.

It has been established that employees want pay systems and promotion policies that they perceive as being just, unambiguous and in line with their expectations. Job satisfaction is enhanced when workers see their pay as being fairly based on job demands, individual skill level and the overall national pay standards. Insufficient pay or perceived inequitable pay is a more decisive determinant of dissatisfaction than sufficient or equitable pay is of satisfaction.

Research studies have shown that people with higher levels occupations tend to be more satisfied with their jobs. People in higher level occupations are better paid and have better working conditions and their jobs make fuller use of their abilities and these in turn make them more satisfied. Evidence from research shows that as we go up the hierarchy, we generally find more satisfied employees. It seems likely that the satisfied employees get more promotions than those employees who are dissatisfied and are always grumbling. Employees seek equitable promotion practice and policies.

Workers are concerned with their work environment for their personal comfort as well as for facilitating efficiency at work. The working environment should have clean, modern and adequate tools and equipment. Studies have also shown that there is an increase in workers' job satisfaction when they have friendly and supportive co-workers and an immediate supervisor who is understanding, friendly and showing personal interest in their employees.

Herzberg et al. averaged the findings of 16 studies involving 11,000 employees where workers were asked to rank-order various aspects of work in terms of their importance.[44] The first ranked factor was security, the second was the interest from intrinsic aspects of the job, the third was opportunity for advancement, and the fourth was considerate and appreciative supervision. Sheppard and Herrick carrying out research two decades after Herzberg, found some changes in the ranking of the job factors by workers. In this study, interesting work was ranked first, enough equipment was ranked second, information was ranked third, authority to get the job done was ranked fourth, good pay was ranked fifth and job security ranked last.

Okumbe, carrying out research on levels of job satisfaction among graduate teachers in secondary schools in Kenya, asked respondents to rank-order eight job factors in their order of importance. The results in this study showed a close similarity with Herzberg's. Job security was ranked first, working conditions and the work environment was ranked second, remuneration was ranked third, work content was ranked fourth, promotion was ranked fifth, interpersonal relations was ranked sixth, management and supervision was ranked seventh and recognition eighth.[45]

An integrated mmotivation model

In this chapter, many theories of worker motivation and job satisfaction have been discussed. It is, however, important to integrate these theories so as to enable the reader to understand their interrelationships.

Figure 6 represents a model which integrates most of the motivation theories. In this model, the important role played by opportunities is emphasised. Opportunities can either aid or hinder individual effort. The arrow leading into the individual effort from the individual's goals shows that goals direct behaviour, in accordance with the goal-setting theory. The arrow from individual effort into individual performance indicates that for an employee's effort to lead to good performance, he or she must have the necessary ability to perform, and that the performance evaluation system must also be seen to be objective. This is in line with the expectancy theory. The performance reward relationship is strengthened if the individual perceives that it is performance, not security, favouritism or other biased criteria, which is rewarded. The model then links the achievement need and equity theories.

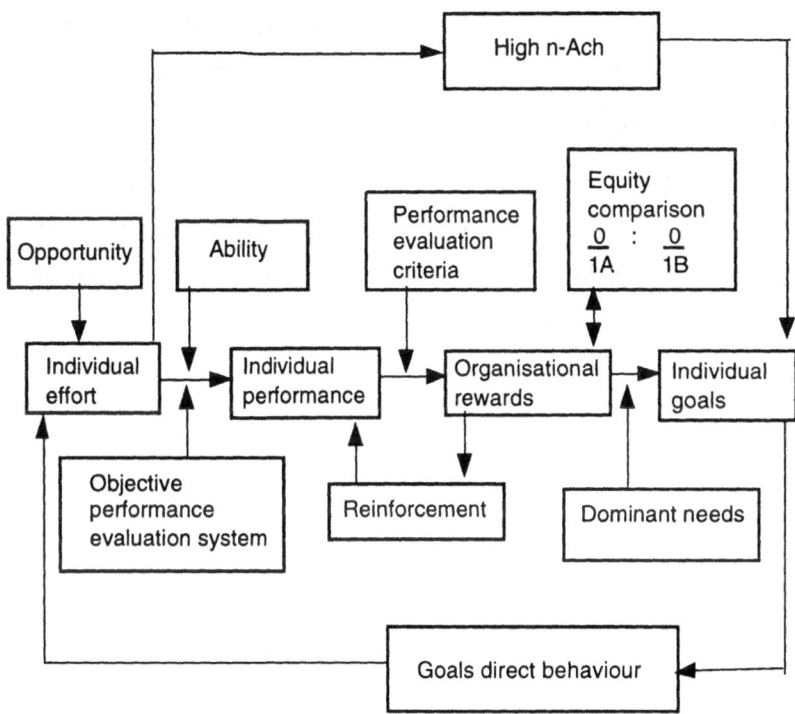

Fig. 6 Integrating contemporary theories of motivation
(Adapted from Stephen P. Robbins, *Organisational Behaviour*, 4th Ed., p. 175.)

Summary

This chapter begins with a distinction between the two closely related concepts of motivation and job satisfaction, followed by a short historical review on the advent of the feelings about motivation and job satisfaction at work.

In the next section both the content and the process theories of motivation and job satisfaction are discussed. The content theories discussed here are the needs-hierarchy, the two-factor, the ERG, McGregor's and McClelland's theories. The process theories discussed are the expectancy, the equity, the goal-setting and the job characteristics theories. In each case the conceptual framework, pertinent research, criticisms as well as applications in educational management are discussed.

Towards the end of the chapter a review of literature on the relationship between job satisfaction and some independent variables has been provided. The chapter ends with an integrated motivational model by Robbins.

END NOTES

[1] F. Luthans, *Organisational Behaviour*, 5th Ed. New York: McGraw-Hill Book Company 1989, p. 23.

[2] Ibid, p. 231.

[3] E.A. Locke, "The nature and cause of job satisfaction", in Dunette, M.D. Ed. *Handbook of Industrial and Organisational Psychology*. Chicago: Rand and McNally, 1976, p. 1300.

[4] J.A. Okumbe, "Levels of job satisfaction among graduate teachers in secondary schools in Siaya District and Kisumu Town", Ph.D. Thesis, University of Nairobi, 1992, p. 27.

[5] C. Miskel and R. Ogawa. "Work motivation, job satisfaction and climate", in Boyan, N.J. (ed.) *Handbook on Research on Educational Administration*. A project of the American Research Association, New York: Longman Inc. 95, 1988. pp. 286-289.

[6] K. Davis and J.W. Newstrom. *Human Behaviour at Work: Organisational Behaviour*. New York; Mc Graw-Hill Book Company, 1985, p. 7.

[7] Ibid.

[8] L.W. Porter, *et. al. Behaviour in Organisations*. New York: McGraw-Hill Book Company 1975, p. 43.

[9] J.P. Campbell, and R.D. Pritchard. "Motivation theory in industrial and organisational psychology", in M.D. Dunette (Ed.), *Handbook of Industrial and Organisational Psychology*. Chicago: Rand-McNally, 1976. pp. 63-130.

[10] M.A. Wahba, and L.G. Bridwell. "Maslow reconsidered. A review of research needs, hierarchy theory," in *Organisational Behaviour and Human Performance*. 15. 1976, 212-240.

[11] G.R. Salancik and J. Pfeffer. "An examination of job attitudes," in *Administrative Science Quarterly*, 9, 1977, p. 453.

[12] L.W. Porter, "Job attitudes in management, perceived importance of needs as a function of job-level," in *Journal Applied Psychology* 47, 1963, 141-148.

[13] F.M. Trusty and T.J. Sergiovani. "Perceived need deficiencies of teachers and administrators' roles," in *Educational Administration Quarterly* 2, 1966, pp. 168-180.

[14] W.C. Hamner and D.W. Organ. *Organisational Behaviour: An Applied Psychological Approach.* Dallas, Texas: Business Publications Inc., 1978, pp. 153-154.

[15] N. King, "Clarifications and evaluation of the two-factor theory of job satisfaction", in *Psychological Bulletin* 74, 1970, 18-31.

[16] R.M. Steers, and L.W. Porter. *Motivation and Work Behaviour*, 2nd Ed. New York: McGraw-Hill Book Co. 1979. pp. 394 - 395.

[17] R.M. Steers, *Introduction to Organisational Behaviour*, 4th Ed. New York: Harper and Collins Publishers Inc., 1991. p. 129.

[18] Luthans, *op. cit.* p. 245.

[19] D.C. McClelland, *The Achieving Society.* Princeton: Van Nostrand Reinhold, 1961.

[20] D.C. McClelland, "Toward a theory of motive acquisition" in *American Psychologist*, 1965, pp. 321-333.

[21] D.P. Schwab, *et al.*, "Between subjects expectancy theory research: A statistical review of studies predicting effort and performance," in *Psychological Bulletin* 86, 1979, 139-147.

[22] L. Festinger, "A theory of social comparison processes," in *Human Relations* 7, 1954, 177-140.

[23] J.S. Adams, "Inequity in social exchange, annual review of psychology", 1968, in Richard M. Steers and Lyman K. Porter, *Motivation and Work Behaviour*, New York: McGraw-Hill Book Company, 1975, p. 141.

[24] D.R. Ilgen and B.W. Hamstra, "Performance satisfaction as a function of the difference between expected and reported performance at five levels of reported performance," in *Organisational Behaviour and Human Performance* 7, 1972, 359-370.

[25] W.C. Hamner and D.L. Harnett, "Goal setting, performance and satisfaction in an independent task", in *Organisational Behaviour and Human Performance* 12, 1974, 217-230.

[26] C.G. Miskel, D. Glasnapp and R.V. Hartleg, "A test of inequity theory for job satisfaction using educators' attitudes toward work motivation and work incentives," in *Educational Administration Quarterly* 11, 1975, 38-54.

[27] W.G. Ortloff, "The use of the equity theory in predicting job satisfaction among high school administrators", in N.J. Boyan, Ed. *op. cit.* p. 288.

[28] R.M. Steers, *Introduction to Organisational Behaviour, op. cit.* p. 155.

[29] F. Luthans, *op. cit.* p. 276.

[30] Ibid.

[31] E.A. Locke, G.P. Latham and M. Erez, "The determinants of goal commitment", in *Academy of Management Review*, Jan. 1988, p. 24.

[32] F. Luthans, *op. cit.* pp. 267-268.

[33] J.R. Hackman and G.R. Oldham, "Motivation through the design of work: A test of a theory", in *Organisational Behaviour and Human Performance* 16, 1976, 250-279.

[34] J.R. Hackman, "Work design", in J.R. Hackman, and J.L. Scuttle (eds). "Improving life at work", in *Good Year*. California: Santa Monica, 1977, p. 129.

[35] F. Luthans, *op. cit.* p. 270.

[36] R. Katz, "Job Longevity as a situational factor in job satisfaction", in *Administrative Science Quarterly* 23, 1978, 204-223.

[37] Miskel and Ogawa, *op. cit.* p. 283.

[38] M.C. Pastor and D.A. Erlandson. "A survey of higher-order need strength and job satisfaction among secondary public school teachers", in *Journal of Educational Administration* 20, 1982, 172-183.

[39] K.R. Garrisson and P.M. Muchinsky, "Attitudinal and biographical predictors", in *Journal of Applied Psychology*, June 1981, pp. 385-389.

[40] S.P. Robbins, *Organisational Behaviour, Concepts and Applications*, 4th Ed. Englewood Cliffs, New Jersey: Prentice Hall, 1989, p. 46.

[41] L.W. Porter, and R.M. Steers, "Organisational work and personal factors in employees' turnover and absenteeism", in *Psychological Bulletin*, Jan. 1973, pp. 151-176.

[42] A.L. Kalleberg and K.A. Loscocco, "Aging values and rewards: explaining age differences in job satisfaction", in *American Social Review*, Feb. 1983.

[43] H.L. Sheppard and N.Q. Herrick, "Where have all the robots gone?" in W.C. Hamner, and D.W. Organ, *Organisational*

Behaviour: An Applied Pschological Approach. Dallas. Texas: Business Publications Inc., 1978, pp. 223-225.

44F. Herzberg, B. Mausner, R. Peterson and D. Capwell, "Job attitudes: review of research and opinion," in Hamner, W.C. and D.W. Organ, *Organisational Behaviour: An Applied Psychological Approach.* Ontario: Business Publications Inc. 1978, pp. 226-227.

45J.A.Okumbe, *op. cit.* p. 259-264.

LEADERSHIP, AUTHORITY AND POWER

This chapter discusses the closely related concepts of leadership, authority and power and shows how they are important ingredients in the efficient achievement of organisational or school goals.

Leadership

Katz and Kahn have defined leadership as the influential increment over and above mechanical compliance with routine directives of the organisation.[1] In this definition, leadership is seen as a process whereby one person influences others to do something of their own volition, neither because it is required nor because of the fear of the consequences of non-compliance. Leadership is thus a process of encouraging and helping others to work enthusiastically toward objectives. It is the human factor that binds a group together and motivates it towards goals by transforming the groups potentials into reality. This voluntary aspect of the response to leadership is what makes it different from authority and power.

Leadership in organisational dynamics fills many of the voids left by conventional organisational designs, allows for greater organisational flexibility and responsiveness to environmental changes, provides a way to coordinate the efforts of diverse groups within the organisation, and facilitates organisational membership and personal needs satisfaction.[2]

Background to studies on leadership

The pioneering leadership studies are known as the "Iowa leadership studies", which were conducted in the late 1930s by Ronald Lippitt and Ralph K. White under the general direction of Kurt Lewin at the University of Iowa.[3] In the first part of the studies, hobby clubs for ten-year-old boys were formed. In each of the clubs the three different leadership styles of authoritarianism, democracy and Laissez faire were applied. The authoritarian leader did not allow the members to participate in decisioin making and was grossly directive. The democratic leader, on the other hand, encouraged members to participate in decisioin making through group discussion. However, the *laissez faire* leader gave members complete freedom, which resulted into no leadership provided to the group.

The three leadership styles were manipulated to show their effects on such variables as satisfaction and frustration. One clear-cut finding in these studies was that the boys had an overwhelming preference for the democratic leader. Nineteen of the twenty boys indicated that they liked the democratic leader more than the authoritarian leader. Seven out of ten boys also chose the laissez faire leader over the authoritarian leader.

The Iowa leadership studies are often discounted on the basis of both their experimental group of pre-dolescent boys instead of adults working in a complex organisation, and the crude research methodology. They, however, were the first to analyse leadership scientifically and they were also the first to show that different styles of leadership can produce different and complex reactions from the same or similar groups.[4]

In 1945, the Bureau of Business Research at Ohio State University initiated a series of studies on leadership.[5] The researchers, who formed an interdisciplinary team from psychology, sociology and economics, developed and applied the leader behaviour description questionnaire (LBDQ). LBDQ was used to analyse leadership in various types of groups and situations. The studies covered a number of armed force personnel, personnel in industry, college administrators, teachers, principals and various leaders of civilian groups.

The LBDQ was administered in a wide variety of situations. The answers to the questionnaire were subjected to factor analysis. The results consistently showed the two dimensions of leadership of *consideration* and *initiating* structure. The Ohio State University factors are task or goal orientation (initiating structure) and recognition of individual needs and relationships (consideration). These two dimensions are distinctly separate. The most important finding of the Ohio State University studies is the "discovery" of both *task* and *human* dimensions in assessing leadership. It is important to note that this two-dimensional approach helped in bridging the gap between the scientific management movement and the human relations movement.

The Early Michigan Leadership Studies were conducted by researchers from the Survey Research Center of the University of Michigan. These studies were conducted at about the same time as the Ohio State University studies. The initial studies were conducted at the Prudential Insurance Company, where twelve high and low productivity pairs were selected for examination. Non-directive interviews were conducted with 24 section supervisors and 419 clerical workers. The results showed that supervisors of high producing sections were significantly likely to be more general than close in their supervisory styles, and be employee-centred. The low-producing section supervisors, on the other hand, showed distinctly opposite characteristics and techniques. Another important finding in this study was that employee satisfaction was not directly related to productivity.

Theories of leadership

The earlier studies of leadership at Iowa, Ohio State and Michigan Universities led to several theoretical bases for leadership studies. These include the trait contingency path-goal and group exchange theories.

The trait theories of leadership

The earliest trait theories of leadership can be traced back to the ancient Greeks and Romans. These early theories believed that leaders are born, not made. This gave rise to the *great man theory*. However, later researchers began to accept that leadership traits are not completely inborn, but can also be acquired through learning and experience. This new thinking on leadership stimulated a lot of research which aimed at determining common traits possessed by leaders. Although a lot of research effort has been expended on this area, the findings have, however, not agreed on the common traits which are found in leaders.

In 1948, Ralph Stogdill reviewed 124 empirical studies on leader attributes covering 27 recurring characteristics. From his review of literature he concluded that leaders exhibited the following characteristics:[6]

(i)   Capacity: Intelligence, alertness, verbal facility, originality, judgement.
(ii) Achievement: Scholarship, knowledge, athletic, accomplishments.
(iii) Responsibility: Dependability, initiative, persistence, aggressiveness, self-confidence, desire to excel.
(iv) Participation: Activities, sociability, cooperation, adaptability, humour.
(v)   Status: Socio-economic position, popularity.
(vi) Situation: Mental level, status, skills, needs and interests of followers, objectives to be achieved.

Stogdill's review also concluded that in many instances the profile of a successful leader varied with the situation.[7] Different groups of workers and different group activities required different types of leaders. This finding by Stogdill shifted the research activities on leadership towards looking into how leaders interacted with groups under various conditions.

Contingency theory of leadership

Since the trait theories failed to provide a comprehensive theoretical framework for leadership, attention was focused on the situational variables that influence leadership roles, skills and behaviour. Whereas the research based on the LBDQ dominated the investigators minds during the 1960s, the contingency theory of leadership, on the other hand, dominated the minds of the researchers in the 1970s. Fred Fiedler is considered as the propelling force in this transformation.[8]

Fiedler's contingency model argues that group performance or effectiveness is dependent upon the interaction of leadership style and the amount of control that the supervisor has over the situation.[9] According to Fiedler, the *situation* in which a leader operates which is the first key variable in the model, can be characterised by three factors.

These factors are:

(i) *Leader-member relations* - Refers to the degree of confidence, trust and respect followers have for the leader.

(ii) *Task structure* - The degree to which the task assignments are clear to both the leader and the subordinates.

(iii) *Position power* - Amount of power attached to the leader's position.

The second key variable in Fiedler's model is the *leader*. He suggests two basic leader orientations. These are:

(i) *Relationship oriented*: which is a more lenient, people oriented style.

(ii) *Task oriented*: which is concerned with the accomplishment of the task.

These two orientations are measured by the least preferred co-worker (LPC) scale. The LPC approach calculates the degree to which leaders favourably perceive worst co-workers and it relates to leadership style. On the LPC scale, an individual is asked to think of the person with whom he or she has worked who was least preferred as a co-worker and to describe this person on several bipolar scales (gloomy-cheerful, tense-relaxed, trustworthy-untrustworthy). If the description of the least preferred co-worker is favourable then this suggests a relationship-oriented leader; an unfavourable description, on the other hand, suggests a task-oriented leader.

When Fiedler combined LPC scores with situation favourableness, he found out that the relationship-oriented leaders were more effective in facilitating group performance when the situation was moderately favourable or moderately unfavourable.[10] On the other hand, the task-oriented leader was more effective in securing group performance when the situation is either highly unfavourable or highly favourable. Figure 7 summarises this.

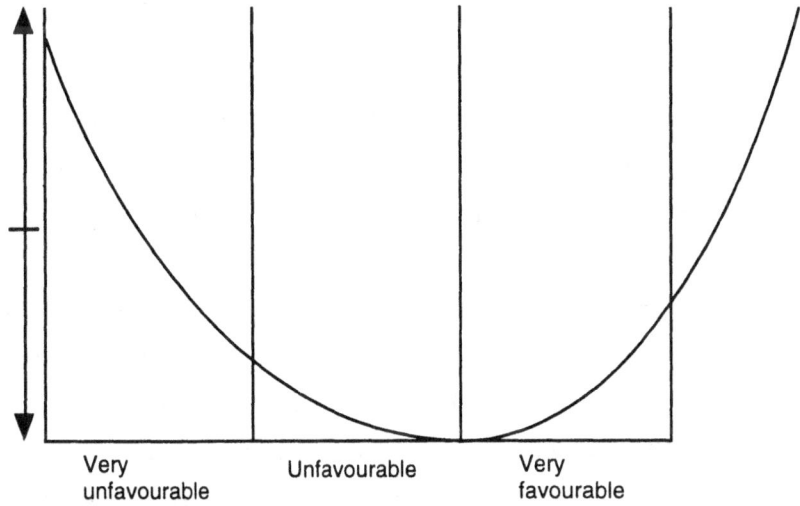

Fig. 7 Fiedler's model of leadership
(Source: Fiedler, Fred E. *Theory of Leadership Effectiveness.* New York: McGraw-Hill Book Company, 1967, pp. 142-148.)

The path-goal leadership theory

The path goal leadership theory has its roots in the expectancy theory. Its theory emphasises on how leaders can facilitate task performance by showing subordinates how performance can be instrumental in achieving desired rewards. The theory argues that people are satisfied with their work and will work hard if they believe that their work will lead to things that are highly valued.[11] The theory emphasises that the managerial behaviour should be motivating or satisfying to the extent that it increases goal attainment by subordinates and clarifies the paths to these goals.[12] The modern development of this theory is usually attributed to Martin Evans[13] and Robert House[14], who wrote separate papers on the subject.

The path-goal theory of leadership rests on two propositions:

1. That the leader behaviour will be acceptable and satisfying when subordinates perceive it to be an immediate source of satisfaction or as being instrumental in obtaining future satisfaction;
2. That leader behaviour will be motivating to the extent that it makes subordinate satisfaction contingent upon effective performance and to the extent that it complements the subordinates' work environment by providing necessary guidance, clarity of direction, and rewards for effective performance.[15]

A comprehensive theory of leadership must recognise at least four distinct types of leader behaviour:[16]

(i) *Directive leadership:* In this type of leadership the subordinates are not active participants since the leader provides them with specific guidance, standards and work plans, including rules and regulations.

(ii) *Supportive leadership:* The leader shows concern for the well being and personal needs of the subordinates. He or she is approachable and friendly.

(iii) *Achievement-oriented leadership:* The leader sets challenging goals and exhibits the confidence that the subordinates will achieve high standards since they are endowed with the requisite potentials.

(iv) *Participative leadership:* In this type of leadership the leader consults with the subordinates and embodies their suggestions in decisioin making.

Figure 8 below summarises the path-goal leadership theory.

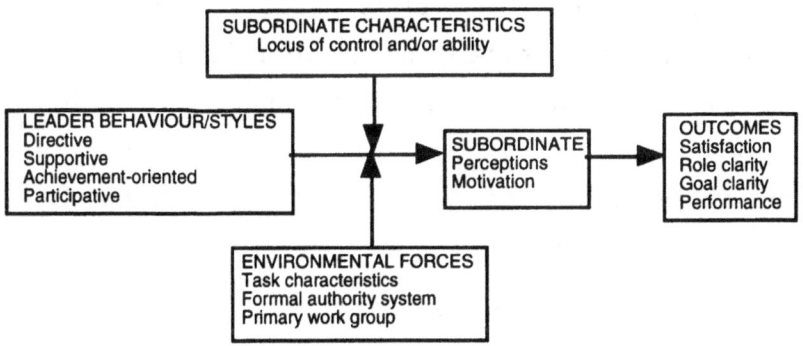

Fig. 8 A summary of the path-goal theory

The path-goal theory stresses that effective leadership is a function of the interaction between leader behaviour and situational or contingency variables of *subordinate characteristics* and *environmental factors*. These contingency factors interact with leader behaviour to determine employee attitudes and behaviour. The employee attitudes and behaviour may be motivated or constrained.

The group and exchange theory of leadership

According to this theory, there must be a positive exchange between the leaders and followers in order for group goals to be accomplished.

The vertical dyad linkage (VDL) model developed by George Graen and his associates is relevant to the exchange theory of leadership.[17] It is sometimes called leader member exchange

(LMX). It states that leaders treat individual subordinates differently. A leader develops a dyadic (two-person) relationship between himself or herself and a subordinate. Over time the leader develops closer interpersonal relationships with some subordinates called the in-group, while keeping his or her distance from other subordinates called the out-group. These different relationships may be due to personal compatibilities or subordinate competence.

Research shows the existence of in-group and out-group relationships with supervisors or leaders.[18] It has also been shown that the in-group members are generally more satisfied and more influential than the out-group members. It is, therefore, important for a leader to recognise the *dyadic relationship* and strive to curb its negative repercussions on workers motivation, satisfaction and performance.

The charismatic theory of leadership

Charismatic leadership theory, also known as transformational leadership theory, says that followers make attributions of heroic or extra-ordinary leadership abilities when they observe certain behaviours.[19] It relies heavily on the trait theory of leadership already discussed. A charismatic leader inspires followers beyond their own self-interests. He or she has an extra ordinary effect on the followers. Charisma as a basis of authority occurs in those instances where a very magnetic personality has been able to capture a following through belief in his mystical, magical, divine or simply extra ordinary powers.[20]

A number of scholars have attempted to identify personal characteristics of the charismatic leaders. Extremely high confidence, dominance and strong convictions in his or her beliefs are characteristics which have been identified by House.[21] A study on charismatic leadership by Conger and Kanungo at McGill University, concludes that charismatic leaders have an idealised goal that they want to achieve, a strong personal commitment to their goal, they are perceived as unconventional, and they are assertive and self confident.[22]

It should, however, be noted that charismatic leaders usually surface in politics, religion or in wartime. In other words, charismatic leadership has more to do with ideological rather than administrative approach.

Leadership styles

A leadership style refers to a particular behaviour applied by a leader to motivate his or her subordinates to achieve the objectives of the organisation. All the various classic leadership theories have direct implications for what style the leader uses in human resource management. Leadership styles are usually identified as points on a continuum.

The democratic, autocratic and laissez faire leadership styles

The pioneering work on leadership conducted at the University of Iowa in 1938 investigated the impact of these three leadership styles on the behaviour of group members.

The democratic leadership, also known as participative or consultative leadership, decentralises power and authority. Decisions are made through consultations. Autocratic leadership style, also known as authoritative, centralises power, authority and decisioin making. In the *laissez faire* case, the leader tends to avoid power and authority; the leader depends largely on the group to establish goals and means for achieving progress and success.

The nomothetic ideographic and transactional leadership styles

These leadership styles were identified and popularised by the Midwest Administrative Center at the University of Chicago.[23] In the *nomothetic leadership* style the leader emphasises the objectives of the organisation and the role of the worker's position. It applies the scientific approach to management. The workers are strictly controlled through the application of rules and regulations stipulated by the organisational structure. It is a task-centred approach to leadership.

The ideographic leadership style, on the other hand, is worker-centred and applies the human relations approach to management. This leadership style emphasises the human dimension of the organisation and is sensitive to the workers' individual needs.

The nomothetic and the ideographic leadership styles are merged together into a *transactional leadership style*. Transactional leadership style varies emphasis on each of the two styles as and when the situation demands.

Leadership training

It is important for educational managers to develop leadership talents that will facilitate organisational effectiveness. In leadership training, attempts are made to develop individuals, like head teachers, principals, supervisors and other people in leadership positions, to their fullest potentials through a variety of training techniques. These training techniques should include general management skills programmes, human relations training, ~oblem solving and decisioin making programmes, and a variety of specialised programmes.[24]

Leadership training of educational managers should enable them to acquire conceptual, human relations and technical skills which are essential in organisational behaviour. In leadership training educational leaders are made through the acquisition of well set out management skills.

Authority

Herbert Simon defines authority as the power to make decisions which guide the actions of another.[25] Authority is legitimate power.

It is power which is vested in a particular person or position, which is recognised by both the wielder of power and by those over whom power is wielded. Authority refers to the ability to influence specified others in accordance with the definitions of certain organisational role relationships. It inheres in the office occupied by an individual and it is his or her right to command, the right to expect obedience and the right to enforce obedience.

Authority is, therefore, the right conferred on an administrator in an organisation to make decisions in the course of discharging his or her responsibilities, to require subordinates to accept the decisions and if necessary to enforce the decisions.[26]

From the foregoing definitions, authority is seen as a relationship between two individuals where one is the superior and the other the subordinate. The decisions are transmitted by the superior to the subordinate who is expected to accept them. The subordinate expects decisions from his superior and it is these decisions which determine his or her conduct. Authority is thus seen in behavioural terms; it takes place only when there is an observable behaviour between the superior and the subordinate. The behaviour of the subordinate is governed by the decision of the superior who selects for him or her the required behaviour pattern. In other words the subordinate holds in abeyance his or her own critical faculties for choosing between alternatives and uses the formal criterion of the receipt of a command or signal as his basis for choice.[27] This is what distinguishes authority from influence. Whereas in authority the subordinate has no choice, in influence a subordinate will make a decision depending upon his or her personal conviction.

Authority performs a number of functions in an organisation. It determines how two individuals who occupy different positions in an organisation relate to each other. Under natural conditions human beings display varied behaviours. Authority thus constitutes a force which reduces human variability in organisations. Individuals must operate consistently within the range of behaviours specified by their rules in organisations.

Authority helps the administrators to enforce a number of house keeping rules, such as no smoking in schools, no wearing of unwanted clothes and no leaving the school compound without permission.

Although it is stressed in the preceding pages that the role of the subordinate is that of a passive implementer of decisions in the superior/subordinate interaction, it should, however, be noted that the subordinate does have a voice at times. A striking characteristic of the subordinate's behaviour is that it establishes *a zone of acceptance of authority* within which the subordinate is willing to accept decisions made for him by the superior. The superior must, therefore, be aware of this zone so that he or she does not go beyond the legally accepted demarcation or boundary.

Types of authority

The *legal* or *formal* authority is a type of authority which has its source in the constitutions, statutes, by-laws and court decisions. Legal authority is divided into: ***Line authority***, which makes decisions of policy and operations, ***staff authority*** which advises, recommends and offers services and ***functional authority*** which is the delegated authority for special purposes. The *technical* or expert authority is the authority that an individual possesses as a result of his or her own extra ordinary ability to do things with a high level of understanding; for instance, a good history teacher, a good educational manager or a good scholar in educational management, are characteristics which people acquire in their professions as a result of their exhibition of extra-ordinary expertise. Expert or technical authority is personal, not institutional; its holder moves with it from one institution to another.

Power

Power is a word which is universally used, and yet its concept has eluded many definitions over the years. One of the earliest definitions of power is that of Max Weber, a German sociologist, who defined power as the probability that one actor within a social relationship will be in a position to carry out his own will despite resistance.[28] Robbins defines power as the capacity that A has to influence the behaviour of B, so that B does something he or she would not otherwise do.[29] Power thus refers to a relationship between two people in which one person has the ability to cause the other to do something which he would otherwise not do.

Classifications of power

The social psychologists, John French and Bertran Raven have identified five categories of power[30]: reward, coercive, legitimate, referent and expert power.

Reward power. This type of power exists when person A has power over person B because A has rewards in his custody which B wants and values. The rewards that A controls include a wide variety of possibilities such as pay raises, promotions, valued job assignments, increased responsibilities, feedback, new equipment and recognition. An educational leader may have a number of rewards at his or her disposal which he or she can use to provide positive reinforcers or valences among teachers, non-teaching staff and students. However, what educational leaders should know is that a reward power is only effective if the subordinates attach importance to the rewards. For instance, a head teacher who provides his or her staff members with a lavish end of term party when the teachers actually think that they need better working and residential conditions instead, does not have reward power in this respect.

Research indicates that reward power often leads to increased job performance since the employees see a strong performance-reward contingency.[31] In educational management, most leadership positions do not provide the incumbent job holders with the requisite reward power which they can use to satisfy and motivate their subordinates. However, intelligent application of such rewards as praise, feedback and more responsibilities do not require money.

Coercive power. This is power which is based primarily on fear. The holder of coercive power has the ability to inflict punishment or negative consequences on the other person. Individuals exercise coercive power through reliance on their physical strength, verbal facility or the ability to grant or withhold emotional support from others.[32] Head teachers and other educational managers have coercive power since they can demote, transfer or sack their subordinates. The importance of coercive power is that it makes people follow rules, directives or policies of an organisation because they know that they will be punished if they do not conform to the stipulations of management. A lot of organisational behaviour such as prompt attendance, looking busy when the superior passes by and strict adherence to rules, can be attributed more to coercive than reward power. Educational leaders should know when to apply coercive power and when to apply reward power.

Legitimate power. Legitimate power is similar to authority. It is the legal power that a person possesses by virtue of his or her position in an organisation. The person over whom this power is wielded knows that the wielder of this power has the legitimate right to do so in a certain domain. A head teacher has legitimate power to assign work to his teachers since he or she has legitimacy due to the official position held. This power is different from coercive and reward power in the sense that it depends on the official position a person holds and not on his or her relationship with the subordinates.

Legitimate power can be derived from three sources. The first source is cultural. The prevailing cultural values on age, sex, education and such like factors will provide certain people with legitimate power. The second source of legitimate power is the accepted social structure, as in the ruling class, organisational hierarchy or a respected family. The third source of legitimate power is derived by people who are either elected or represent powerful personalities or groups. Chairmen of boards of governors or university councils derive their power this way.

Expert power. Expert power is possessed by a person when people see him or her as having knowledge or expertise which is greatly valued by them. Teachers and professors have expert power in the classroom because of both their mastery and delivery of a particular subject matter. An educational manager who applies his or her management skills appropriately, as and when relevant, has expert power in educational leadership.

Although expert power is the most tenuous type of power, a number of educational leaders like those performing staff functions and thus seldom have other sources of power available to them, usually have to depend on their expertise as their only source of power. Lecturers and teachers derive most of their power from this source.

Referent power. This power is wielded by a person when he or she has personal qualities, characteristics or reputation which others want to be identified with. For instance, marketing managers take advantage of this power when they ask celebrities to do advertising for their products. In an organisational setting, managers posses referent power if they are personally attractive to subordinates. Referent power requires articulate, domineering, physically imposing or charismatic qualities.

Power: A contingency model

The application of power in an organisation is contingent upon three variables: the manager, the subordinate and the organisation itself. Y.R. Shetty has pointed out several specific manager, subordinate and organisational characteristics which are important to a contingency analysis of managerial power.[33] These are summarised in Figure 9. For a manager to be successful he or she must be aware of the existence of multiple sources of power in work situations and that effectiveness of each power type depends on the nature of managerial, subordinate and organisational variables.

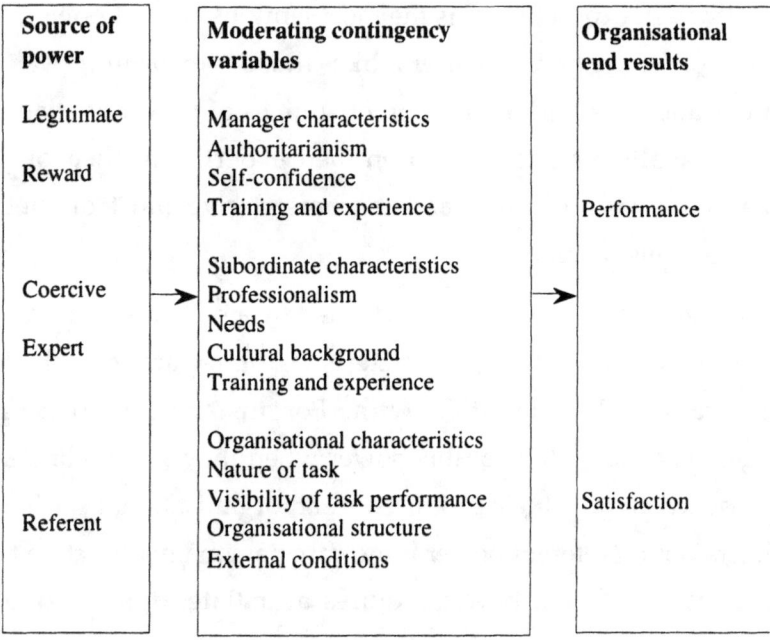

Fig. 9 A contingency model of power types
Source: Adapted from V.K. Shetty, "Managerial power and organisational effectiveness: A contingency analysis" in *Journal of Management Studies*, May 1978, 184.

Application of power in educational management

The use of power in educational organisations, like other organisations in general, is a fact of management which employees must accept. Teachers and other employees in educational organisations however have a right to know that power must be applied by leaders in such a manner that complies with ethical standards which prevent any form of abuse.

An educational manager who applies legitimate power should ensure that he or she is confident, cordial, polite and follows proper channels. In the application of reward power, an educational manager should verify teachers, compliance with work directives. The rewards offered should be the ones valued by the teachers and these should be accurately tied to performance.

The most loathed coercive power can be applied effectively without jeopardising good leaderships. In applying coercive power the educational manager ensures teachers and other educational workers are well informed about rules, regulations and penalties for infractions in advance. Subordinates should be warned before any punishment is meted out, and any punishment must be administered consistently and uniformly in the organisation. Punishment must be in accordance with the magnitude of the offence, and such punishment must be in private.

In applying the referent power, an educational manager ensures that he or she projects a model role that teachers and other subordinates would be willing to be associated with. Sensitivity to subordinates needs and feelings are very important and their interests should be carefully protected by their leader. An educational manager applies expert power by maintaining credibility among the subordinates and by being confident and decisive in his or her management techniques. He or she should be well informed in both education and management theory and practice.

Power and politics in educational organisations

Politics in an organisation refers to "those activities taken within the organisations to acquire, develop and use power and other resources to obtain one's preferred outcomes in a situation in which there is uncertainty or dissensus about choices".[34] A political behaviour in an organisation is an activity which is initiated by a leader so as to overcome opposition and resistance. Such political activities would be non-existent if there were no opposition.

There are a number of reasons for political behaviour in organisations in general and educational organisations in particular. One of the reasons is that of *ambiguous goals*. When the goals of a school or a department are ambiguous, an avenue is created for politics. Due to this some educational leaders would undertake activities which promote their personal gains under the guise of school goals.

The second reason for political behaviour in organisations is the *scarcity of resources*. There is a direct relationship between the amount of politics and the scarcity of resources in an organisation. For instance, if a number of departments have to fight for limited funds, office space, scholarships and hiring of new personnel, then there develops an intensive infighting between departments so that each can claim its "share". Similarly, availability of extra or unclaimed resources may also create political behaviour.

The third reason for political behaviour is the presence of *ambiguous (non-programmed) decisions*. Ambiguous decisions create a lot of uncertainties among educational managers and this leaves room for political behaviour between departments.

The fourth reason for political behaviour is the *changing technology and environment*. Political behaviour is increased when the internal technology of an educational organisation is non-routine and the societal environment is dynamic and complex. This increases uncertainty and ambiguities and different educational managers will be interested in pursuing their desired courses of action.

The fifth reason for political behaviour in organisations is *organisational change*. When an educational organisation is restructuring itself by, for instance, creating a new department or a course, or totally changing its level of training through curriculum change, different factions and coalitions begin to fight over "territorial integrity".

Educational managers should thus be aware of these political processes within educational settings and apply leadership techniques which will eliminate or minimise their adverse effects on performance. It is possible to minimise the negative effects of political behaviour by applying rational policies and standard operating procedures in individual organisations.

In this section, we have looked at political behaviour within an educational organisation. However, the reader may be interested in knowing the implication of national or state politics on the management of educational organisations. The implications of the national or state politics on educational management in general follow the same pattern as has been discussed above.

Leadership, authority and power: A clarification

There is no doubt that the concepts of leadership, authority and power are related. However, educational managers should be able to note the existing differences so as to be able to apply them both appropriately and effectively.

Leadership has been seen as the ability one individual has to elicit response from another person that goes beyond expected or mechanical compliance with routine directives. This *voluntariness* in behaviour between a *leader* and the subordinate is what makes leadership different from authority and power. An educational manager who applies his or her leadership skills strives to inspire certain actions within the workers.

Authority, on the other hand, is the right to seek compliance from others. It is backed by legitimacy. A head teacher who commands a teacher to do an assigned work has the legitimate authority to do so. If the teacher refuses to do an assigned work then the stipulated disciplinary procedures which regulate his or her professional conduct can be appropriately applied. Authority is the official way of regulating behaviour in an organisation. In the case of power, the person who possesses it has the ability to *manipulate* or change others. A headteacher who makes school workers to run his or her personal errands applies power and not authority since this is outside the official exercise of authority.

Summary

This chapter begins with an analysis of leadership: background studies, theories, styles and training. Five theories of leadership have been identified and discussed here. These are the trait, contingency, path-goal, group-exchange and charismatic theories. On the leadership styles, the democratic, autocratic, *laissez faire*, nomothetic, ideographic and transactional styles have been discussed. On leadership training, the chapter argues that educational leaders are made through the acquisition of well set out management skills.

The chapter has also provided an in-depth treatise on authority, power and politics in educational organisations. On authority, the legal (formal), line, staff, functional and technical authorities were identified. The discussion on power shows five types of power, namely: reward, coercive, legitimate, expert and referent. The emergence of power and politics in educational management, elucidated. In this section, a distinction has been made between leadership, authority and power.

END NOTES

[1] D. Katz, and R. Kahn. *The Social Psychology of Organisations.* New York: Wiley, 1978, p. 528.

[2] R.M. Steers, *Introduction to Organisational Behaviour,* 4th Ed. New York: Harper Collins Publishers, Inc. 1991, p. 375.

[3] F. Luthans, *Organisational Behaviour,* 5th Ed., New York: McGraw-Hill Book Co., 1989, p. 453.

[4] Ibid, p. 454.

[5] Ibid.

[6] R.M. Stogdill, "Personal factors associated with leadership" in *Journal of Psychology,* 1948, 25, 35-71.

[7] R.M. Steers, *op. cit.* pp.378-79.

[8] E.M. Hanson, *Educational Administration and Organisational Behaviour.* Boston: Allyn and Bacon, Inc. 1979, p. 247.

[9] R.M. Steers, *op. cit.,* p. 380.

[10] Ibid, pp. 382-383.

[11] E.M. Hanson, *op. cit.* p. 254.

[12] R.M. Steers, *op. cit.,* p. 386.

[13] M. Evans, "The effects of supervisor behaviour on the path-goal relationship", in *Organisational Behaviour and Human Performance* 5, 1970, 277-98.

[14] R. House, "A path-goal theory of leadership", in *Administrative Science Quarterly,* 16, 1970, 321-338.

[15] R.M. Steers, *loc. cit.*

[16] M. House, *op. cit.*

[17] G. Graen, F. Dansereau and W. Hage, "A vertical dyad linkage approach to leadership in formal organisations", in *Organisational Behaviour and Human Performance,* Feb. 1975, 46-78.

[18]Ibid.

[19]S.P. Robbins, *op. cit.* p. 329.

[20]E.H. Schein, "Organisational psychology", in D.M. Mbiti, *Foundations of School Administration*, Nairobi: Oxford University Press, 1982 p. 34.

[21]R.J. House, "A 1976 theory of charismatic leadership", in J.G. Hunt and I.L. Larson (eds), *Leadership: The Cutting Edge*. Carbondale, Southern Illinois University Press, 1977, pp. 189-207.

[22]J.A. Conger, and R.N. Kanungo. "Toward a behavioural theory of charismatic leadership in organisational settings", in *Academy of Management Review*, October 1987, 637-647.

[23]Hanson, *op. cit.* p. 242.

[24]R.M. Steers, *op. cit.* p. 396.

[25]H.A. Simon, "Authority" in Robert Dubin, (ed.) *Human Relations in Administration*, 4th Ed. Englewood Cliffs, New Jersey: Prentice Hall, 1974 p. 329.

[26]D.M. Mbiti, *Foundations of School Administration*. Nairobi: Oxford University Press, 1982, p. 25.

[27]Tead Ordway, *Human Nature and Management*. New York: McGraw-Hill Book Co. Inc. 1929 p. 149.

[28]Max. Weber, "The theory of social and economic organisations", in R.M. Steers, *op. cit.* p. 482.

[29]S.P. Robbins, *Organisational Behaviour, Concepts and Applications*, 4th Ed. Englewood Cliffs, New Jersey: Prentice Hall, 1989 p. 339.

[30]John R.P. French Jr., and Bertram Raven. "The bases of social power", in D. Cartwright (ed.), *Studies in Social Power*, University of Michigan, Institute for Social Research, Ann Arbor, 1959.

[31] Y. Shetty, "Managerial power and organisational effectiveness: A contingency analysis", in *Journal of Management Studies* 5, 1978, 178-181.
[32] R.M. Steers, *op. cit.* p. 485.
[33] Y.K. Shetty, *op. cit.* p. 184.
[34] P. Pfeffer, *Power in Organisations*. Marshfield, Mass: Pitman, 1981, p. 7.

Chapter Five

DISCIPLINE

Discipline is the action by management to enforce organisational standards.[1] In an educational organisation, there are many standards or codes of behaviour to which teachers, students and non-teaching staff must adhere.

In order to successfully achieve the objectives of a school, college or University, all the members of the educational organisation are required to strictly adhere to the various behaviour patterns necessary for maximum performance. In Chapter Four we have learned what goes into effective management and what an educational manager requires in order to be an effective leader. Despite the acquisition and application of the theoretical skills required of a leader, educational managers will still be faced with cases of teachers, students and non-teaching staff who do not strictly follow the set standards of their educational organisations. It is thus imperative that educational managers use appropriate disciplinary action to maintain organisational standards necessary for optimum goal attainment.

Types of Discipline

There are two types of discipline, namely, preventive discipline and corrective discipline.

Preventive discipline

This is the administrative action taken by an educational manager to encourage employees and students to follow the standards, rules and regulations which prevent infractions. The principle in preventive discipline is to instil self-discipline among the organisational participants. The educational managers should strive to attain self-discipline within their organisations since this vases morale and therefore productivity.

In order to encourage preventive discipline, educational managers should provide an enabling organisational climate in which expected standards are stated positively.

Corrective discipline

This the administrative action which follows an infraction of a rule. Corrective discipline is aimed at discouraging further infringement of a rule. The administrative action meted out is a *disciplinary action*. Educational managers should strive to minimise, if not eliminate, corrective discipline by strengthening preventive discipline; they should understand the basic tenets of a disciplinary action. These are to reform the offender, to deter others from similar actions, and to maintain consistent effective group standards.[2]

Educational managers should be able to apply disciplinary actions in a progressive manner in what is known as *progressive discipline*. A progressive discipline follows a procedure which proceeds from an oral warning to a written warning to a suspension and finally to a dismissal.[3] The main purpose of progressive discipline is to give an employee the opportunity for self correction before more serious penalties are imposed.[4] Progressive discipline also enables an educational manager and an employee enough time for remedial actions which ensure employee's conformity to the set standards.

Two Views of Discipline

There are two opposing views on discipline and these are in line with Douglas McGregor's theory X and theory Y assumptions about people, as discussed in Chapter Three.

Theory X view about discipline

Educational managers who look at discipline only as a punishment are applying theory X assumptions about people. These assumptions are enumerated in Chapter Three.

Although theory X assumptions about people are viewed as being negative and, therefore, autocratic, there are cases when workers have to be treated as prescribed by theory X. For instance, there are cases where a teacher, a student or a non-teaching member of staff just does not want to follow the set code of behaviour in an educational organisation despite the application of the various leadership skills by the supervisor. In such a case a disciplinary action should take the theory X assumption.

Educational managers who take the above theory X view about teachers, students and non-teaching staff will use discipline as a means to enforce external demands for responsible behaviour. Such leaders do not recognise the importance of self discipline and will, therefore, expect orderly behaviour to depend mainly on fear of penalties. Discipline is thus exercised as a punishment to both deter and retribute the offenders. This approach is a negative view about people in their work places and is an autocratic approach to enforcing organisational standards.

Theory Y view about discipline

Educational managers who look at discipline as a process of encouraging workers to move uniformly towards meeting the objectives of education are applying the theory Y assumptions about people (see Chapter Three).

Educational managers who take the theory Y approach to discipline strive to provide intelligent leadership in their organisations so that maximum potentials can be released from their subordinates. Such leaders thus use discipline as an effective by-product of efficient application of leadership skills so as to gain willing cooperation from teachers, students and other workers within the rules and regulations set by the educational management and duly accepted by all members in the organisation. The main aim of this approach is to inculcate among all organisational members a voluntary self-discipline. This approach takes a positive view about discipline.

However, as already stated earlier, a few people in an organisation will fail to comply with established rules and standards even after repeated appeals by the management. The organisational rules and standards are more applicable to such workers than to the majority who have acquired self-discipline. All educational managers should thus see the primary purpose of discipline as being that of supplementing and strengthening self-discipline among the individuals and the entire work group of teachers, students and other workers.

Principles of Setting Good Disciplinary Actions

The principles of setting good disciplinary actions follow McGregor's "hot stove rule" in which McGregor emphasises that a good disciplinary action should follow precisely the consequences of a burn from a hot stove; that is, before you touch a hot stove you have already been *warned* by the fire. When you touch the hot stove you will be burnt *immediately*, and this burning will be *consistent* each time you touch the hot stove. Finally the burning will be *impersonal*, regardless of your size, position, age or even sex.

The following principles stem from McGregor's hot stove rule:

There should be prior knowledge of rules and regulations. The educational manager must ensure that all staff members (teaching and non-teaching) are informed about the terms and conditions of their employment, and the rules and regulations of the organisation in which they work. This should be done during orientation or induction. The students should also be well informed about the organisation's rules and the consequences of breaking them. The rules should be clear and copies given to both staff and students. Often, new rules are made or old ones are modified as situations dictate, and this should be communicated to the relevant people promptly.

A more useful and effective method of communicating the rules and regulations is the use of a handbook. Such handbooks should spell out the rules of conduct, the reasons for the rules and also the consequences of not following these rules.

A disciplinary action should be applied immediately. All the infractions should be dealt with immediately regardless of their magnitude. Educational managers must ensure that any undesirable behaviour by either the staff members or students is dealt with immediately so that the offenders can see the close connection between an undesirable behaviour and its consequence. When there is a long time lapse between the undesirable behaviour and its consequence then the association between the two becomes weak and this provides a stimulus for more undesirable behaviour.

Disciplinary actions must be consistently applied. This is to say that educational managers should ensure that similar offences are dealt with in similar ways. If there are variations in the way similar offences are dealt with in an organisation, there is the likelihood of a general workers discontent which may lead to a revolt. It is important to follow past precedents. A fair disciplinary action demands that the educational manager who is administering the disciplinary action does not show any favouritism. An inconsistent application of a disciplinary action may do more harm than good to an organisation by inadvertently reinforcing an undesirable behaviour.

Disciplinary actions must be objective. An effective disciplinary action must be based on facts, not inferences. An educational manager must, therefore, carry out a thorough research to ensure that the offence was actually committed by the said staff or student before a disciplinary action is taken.

Disciplinary actions should be impersonal. An educational manager must be aware that it is the undesirable action which is being punished and not the person. A good disciplinary action should neither be used for revenge nor as a chance to vent frustrations.[5] An educational leader should not carry the punishment over. Once a staff member or a student has been punished for an offence, normal relations must be reinstated immediately as if this incident had not occurred.

Avoid entrapment. Those who break the regulations of an educational organisation should be punished for what they have actually done but not what they could have done!

Allow right of appeal. The right of appeal is a very important ingredient of a democratic disciplinary process. Staff and students must be allowed to defend themselves against the offence for which they have been charged. Otherwise somebody may be punished for an offence which he or she never committed or for something whose circumstances were unavoidable.

The Disciplinary Process

It is important that an effective educational management stipulates, in writing, the disciplinary procedure which gives details about how the actions will proceed. A systematic, effective disciplinary action should follow the following procedure:

Preliminary investigation

When a teacher, student or any other worker fails to meet the standards of behaviour as stipulated in an educational organisation, the first step should be to investigate the case thoroughly. This will enable the leader to find out whether this is a first offence or another in a series, or whether there are underlying reasons for the offence like ill-health, family problems, or whether this is a way by which an employee is expressing his or her dissatisfaction with the job or the school. If the educational manager takes a hasty disciplinary action against a worker or a student without getting the relevant background information, then the consequences could be too serious to be solved easily. Skilful interviewing is needed, not in a spirit of cross examination, but in an effort to understand why the employee acted the way he or she did.[6]

If the preliminary investigation does not promptly reveal all the facts of the case which may help the educational manager to decide whether a disciplinary action is necessary or not, then the next step is temporary suspension of the teacher, student or worker.

Temporary suspension

Temporary suspension or interdiction is very important in helping the educational management to gain enough time for thorough investigations. It helps a leader to act promptly, perhaps in a situation that could become explosive and where a serious penalty may prove to be justified, but where key facts have not yet been established.[7] During the period in which a suspect is temporarily suspended, there is enough time for the management to look into the facts systematically and in a calm atmosphere. Temporary suspension thus helps both the management and the suspects. A temporary suspension in itself is not a punishment until the verdict of the investigation is given.

When a teacher, student or any other worker is temporarily suspended he or she should promptly leave the premises of the organisation until the case is finalised.

Oral warning/reprimand and written warning/reprimand

When the preliminary investigations in the first step are concluded and the offence committed does not warrant temporary or permanent removal from the organisation, then either an oral warning/reprimand or written warning/reprimand can be undertaken.

In the case of an *oral warning* or *reprimand* an educational manager believes that a deviant behaviour can still be changed through a private discussion. A favourable time and a *private* place should be set for this. The aim is to inform the staff or student that the undesirable behaviour cannot be tolerated and, therefore, there is an urgent need for improvement, failing which a serious disciplinary action will be administered. An oral reprimand is effective if it is given in a skilful and friendly manner. However, if it is given in an unfriendly manner, for instance in public, it may provoke hostility and defensive behaviour.

A written warning or reprimand in most cases should follow an oral warning. If a teacher or student does not respond positively to the oral talks in private, then a written warning is issued. In some cases the offence committed is too strong for the oral warning, in which case a written warning is administered. The written warning should contain a statement of the offence committed with copies of letters sent to the relevant officers who deal with the offender's employment or academic record. Usually it is expected that a written warning should be preceded by either a friendly talk during counselling or an oral warning.

Although the importance of both oral and written warnings have been stressed, it is sometimes useful for an educational manager to have infrequent *informal* but *friendly* talks with staff at personal levels because this may help to forestall an unbecoming behaviour. This helps to highlight important issues which workers may take for granted.

Demotion, suspension, and discharge from employment

The verdict by a disciplinary committee during the time an employee or a student is temporarily suspended could either be that the suspect is not guilty and should continue with his or her normal work or studies, or the committee may find the suspect guilty. In the case where the suspect is found guilty, the disciplinary measure to be undertaken must be recommended by the committee in accordance with the magnitude of the offence. These measures include demotion, suspension or discharge from employment or studies as the case may be. The disciplinary action recommended should, however, take into account both the seriousness of the offence and whether this is a first, second or third offence.

It is important that educational managers become thoroughly conversant with the disciplinary procedures to be undertaken and to ensure that they are administered both humanely and skilfully. A disciplinary action may mean a great loss to both the worker and the organisation if it is inadvertently handled. The suspect on the other hand is expected to exercise his or her right by appealing against a disciplinary action which is deemed unjustified, so that any disciplinary action is seen to be fair to both the management and the suspect.

Summary

This chapter begins by defining discipline and then proceeded to show that discipline is an issue despite the management's skill in ensuring adherence to strict organisational standards. Two types of discipline, namely, preventive discipline and corrective discipline, have been discussed. The idea of progressive discipline has also been discussed.

The next part of the chapter has discussed theory X and theory Y views about discipline. This is followed by seven principles of good disciplinary action. Finally, the last part of the chapter discusses the disciplinary process in detail.

END NOTES

[1] B.P. Heshizer, and H. Graham. "Discipline in the non-union company protecting employer and employee rights," in *Personnel*, March-April 1982, 71-78.

[2] K. Davis, and J.W. Newstrom. *Human Behaviour at Work: Organisational Behaviour.* New York; Mc Graw-Hill Book Company, 1985, p. 365.

[3] W.F. Cascio, *Managing Human Resources: Productivity, Quality of Work Life, Profits.* New York: McGraw-Hill Inc., 1992, p. 513.

[4] K. Davis, and J.W. Newstrom. *op. cit.* p. 367.

[5] R.A. Baron, and J. Greenberg. *Behaviour in Organisations*, 3rd Ed. Boston: Allyn and Bacon, 1989, p. 63.

[6] P. Pigors and C.A. Myers. *Personnel Administration: A Point of View and a Method.* New York: McGraw-Hill Book Company, 1973, pp. 332-35.

[7] Ibid.

COMMUNICATION

Human beings spend nearly 70 per cent of their waking hours communicating, either by speaking, listening, reading or writing. Although communication is one of the most frequently discussed dynamics in the entire field of organisational behaviour, it is not very well understood.[1]

Definition

In this book the operating definition of communication is that it is the "exchange of information and the transmission of meaning".[2] It is only when meaning is transmitted from one person to another that information and ideas can be conveyed. The meaning must not just be transmitted, it must also be understood. Communication, therefore, involves both transference and understanding of meaning. It is a personal process that involves the exchange of behaviours. The only means by which one person can influence another is by the behaviours he or she performs, that is to say, the communicative exchanges between people provide the sole method by which influence or effects can be achieved.[3]

In management practice, effective communication is a basic prerequisite for the attainment of organisational goals, and yet it has remained one of the biggest problems facing modern management.[4] However great an idea is, it is practically useless until it is transmitted and understood by others who are concerned with it. In "a perfect communication", a thought or an idea is transmitted so that the mental picture perceived by the receiver is exactly the same as that envisioned by the sender.[5] In practice, however, perfect communication is never achieved due to communication barriers which are discussed later in this chapter.

Role of Communication in Educational Management

Communication plays four major roles in educational management:

1. Communication helps to *control the behaviour* of teachers, students and non-teaching staff in a number of ways. For instance, it is through communication that teachers and other staff members are inducted into the various aspects of their jobs and other organisational and employment regulations. Through communication, the students are likewise informed about their *expected behaviour* within the educational organisation. The consequences of deviant behaviour are also specified and understood through communication.

2. Communication helps to *motivate* teachers, students and other workers in an educational organisation. Through communication all members in an educational organisation are informed about what is to be done, how well they are performing their variously assigned tasks and what can be undertaken to make the tasks be done even better. This is done through proper feedback mechanisms.

3. Communication provides a release for the *emotional expression* of feelings and for fulfilment of social needs.[6] For teachers, students and other workers an educational organisation or a work group provides a primary source of their social interaction. It is through communication in the work place that people show their satisfaction, or share their feelings of frustration, with both their work-related activities and social aspects of their lives.
4. Communication facilitates decisioin making. Communication provides teachers and others with the *information* which they require for making appropriate decisions.

Interpersonal Communication

Interpersonal communication refers to communication which is primarily between two individuals. Through interpersonal communication, employees at all levels of an organisation interact with others, secure desired ends, request or extend support, and make use of, and reinforce the formal design of the organisation.[7]

An interpersonal communication model

Although a model helps to outline the basic process involved in a dyadic communication exchange, it is an oversimplification of what really happens in a real life situation. A simplified interpersonal communication model consists of a communicator who encodes and sends a message to a receiver who decodes it and responds in some way, either verbally or behaviourally.[8] Figure 10 shows a basic model of communication.

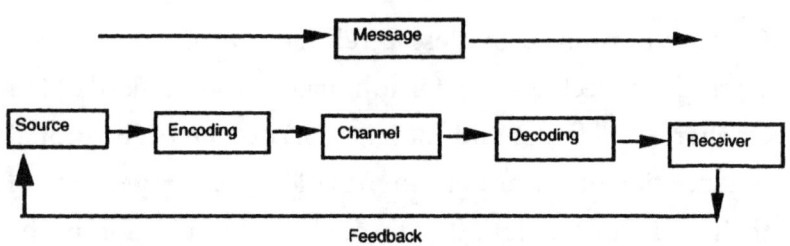

Fig. 10 A basic interpersonal communication model

The source or sender *encodes* the message by translating ideas into a systematic set of symbols or language. The encoded message is affected in four ways. In the first instance, if the source (sender) does not have the requisite skills then the message will not reach the receiver in the form required. Secondly, the attitude of the sender will influence his or her behaviour since different people hold predispositions of ideas on various topics or issues. Thirdly, the source's knowledge about the topic or issue affects the encoded message. The message will be affected by both *too* little and *too* much knowledge. Fourthly, the socio-cultural system within which the source operates will affect the encoded message. This is because the beliefs and values people attach to ideas are influenced by their socio-cultural background.

The transmitted message is *decoded* by the receiver when he or she interprets it. The receiver attaches meaning to the message so that the intention is fully understood. The receiver's decoding ability depends on his or her skills, attitudes, knowledge and the socio-cultural system. The *message* is the actual physical product from the source. It is in the form of speech, writing, painting or gesture. The message we transmit is affected by the code or group of symbols we use to transfer meaning, the content of the message itself, and the decisions that the source makes in selecting and arranging both codes and content.[9] The message passes through a *channel*, which is the medium through which the message is transmitted. The channel is either formal, when it is established by the organisational structure, or informal, when it is not the official medium.

Feedback forms the final link in the process of communication. It helps in evaluating how successful the message has been transmitted as was originally intended. Feedback takes the form of verbal response, gesturing, questioning or no response at all.

Three basic types of feedback have been suggested.[10] These are ***informational corrective and reinforcing.*** In *informational* feedback, the receiver simply provides information to the source. For instance, an educational manager may want to know how many students registered for a particular subject or course. In the *corrective* feedback the receiver responds by giving his or her opinion about the message. In *reinforcing* feedback the receiver acknowledges the receipt of the message by responding either positively, if the message is good, or negatively if the message is bad.

Feedback plays a very important role in communication. It is imperative for the sender to establish both formal and informal mechanisms through which it can be established how the message was interpreted by the receiver. The feedback mechanism makes communication a two-way process. An effective feedback should be specific in providing information, be well intended, descriptive rather than evaluative, well timed, clearly understood, reliable and valid, useful in providing the needed information for the receiver, and applied when the receiver is ready to receive it.

Types of interpersonal communication

There are three main types of interpersonal communication:

1.   *Oral communication*

Oral communication consists of all messages which are spoken. It is by far the most frequently used type of communication.

2.   *Written communication*

Written communication includes letters, reports, notices, manuals and advertisements Written communication is very important where precision of language and message documentation are necessary.

3.   *Non-verbal communication*

Non-verbal communication or the silent language can be defined as "non-word human responses and the perceived characteristics of the environment through which the human verbal and non-verbal messages are transmitted."[11]

There are two forms of non-verbal communication. The first form is the **physical** or **symbolic language**. This includes sirens, traffic lights, status symbols like a big office or a car. The second form is the *body language*, which includes facial expressions, posture, or eye movements.

Although non-verbal communication has had very little research and scholarly interest, it plays a very important role in the communication process. For instance, the amount of time allocated to talking to someone, the amount of office space, the kind of dress, the physical appearance, the employment titles and the interpersonal interactions are very important aspects of non-verbal communication.[12]

Factors influencing interpersonal communication

There are four main factors which influence the interpersonal communication.

1. *Social influence.* Since communication is a social process, a variety of social factors can influence the accuracy of the message which is communicated. For instance, in a school the status barriers between employees at different levels influence their behaviour. The different roles played by different people in a school system will dictate the mode of behaviour between two people.

2. *Employee's perceptual processes.* The accuracy with which a teacher receives instructions from the head teacher or any supervisor will depend on the teacher's opinion about the supervisor giving the instruction. If the head teacher or the supervisor is looked at as an incompetent leader, then the instructions will not be taken seriously; likewise, a serious-minded leader will always be taken seriously.

3. *Interaction involvement.* This refers to the extent to which one or both parties are involved in the communication process. It is important for both parties to be effectively involved in the communication process for the effective transmission of the message.

4. *Organisation design.* The way an organisation is designed has a major influence on the interpersonal communication. In an organisation with many levels or hierarchies, the message is likely to be distorted as it passes through the various levels due to a number of reasons. In a decentralised organisation, the distortion of the message is reduced.

Organisational Communication

Organisational communication refers to communication which takes place among groups of people within organisations. In organisational communication the organisational structure is imposed on the natural patterns of interpersonal relationships.

In organisational communication, there are three general directions in which a message can flow. These are:

(i) Downward;
(ii) Upward; and
(iii) Horizontal.

Downward communication

Downward communication is used by educational managers to direct and influence the activities of teachers and others who occupy the lower hierarchical levels. It is a superior-subordinate communication. Downward communication helps educational managers to:

(i) give specific task directives about job instructions;
(ii) give information about school procedures and practices;
(iii) provide information about the rationale of the teaching job;

(iv) tell teachers, students and other workers about their performance;
(v) help in the socialisation and indoctrination of the teachers, students and other workers.

Downward communication in an educational setting relies on both written and oral media for information dissemination. The written media include school handbooks, manuals, newsletters, bulletin-board notices, posters and memos. The oral media include meetings, speeches, telephones and direct verbal orders from superiors. To improve the effectiveness of downward communication, educational managers must combine both written and oral media in an appropriate manner. Although it has been found out from research studies that oral methods only are more effective than written methods only, it is important for educational managers to combine both methods for effective downward communication.

The effectiveness of downward communication can also be improved by having an effective feedback mechanism which reduces the "filtering effect" which the message goes through when it passes down the various hierarchical levels.

Upward communication

Upward communication is used by educational managers to receive feedback from teachers, students and other workers. It helps educational managers to know what the various people in the educational organisation, students, teachers and non-teaching staff feel about their organisation in terms of both progress and areas needing improvement. Upward communication is a subordinate-superordinate communication.

Some of the examples of upward communication include performance reports prepared by heads of departments and others occupying lower cadres, grievance procedures for collective bargaining agreements, open-door policy, participative techniques as in participative decisioin making, suggestion boxes and employee attitude surveys. Through upward communication subordinates can provide educational managers with information about their personal ideas, attitudes and performance. Subordinates also use upward communication to provide technical feedback information about the educational organisation's performance in terms of meeting its objectives through the various human and material resources necessary for the operation of the organisation.

Horizontal (lateral) communication

Horizontal or lateral communication is the type of communication which takes place among members of work groups at the same level. It is used for co-ordinating activities or projects between departments or units. Horizontal communication, first recognised by Henri Fayol, in the Fayol's Bridge helps to increase the *communication speed* by short-circuiting the formal hierarchical structure of an organisation.

Horizontal communication is about people and their behaviour. Because of this, it is also referred to as *interactive* communication. People usually find it easier and more comforting to communicate with their peers, because these are people with relatively equal status and are on more or less similar levels in the organisation. It is easier to turn to one's peer than to someone below or above one in the organisational hierarchy for support. The horizontal communication may be good for an organisation if the peer communication is for task coordination in order to achieve organisational goals, or it may be bad for the organisation if the peer communication is concerned with things which negate the organisational goals.

Horizontal communication is very important in organisations because it helps departments or departmental heads to coordinate tasks, solve problems, share information and resolve conflicts.

Communication networks

A communication network shows the pattern of interpersonal communication among members of a group or an organisation. Communication networks are combinations of downward, upward and horizontal communications. Five communication networks have been identified. These are the chain, wheel, "Y", circle and all channel (see Figure 11).

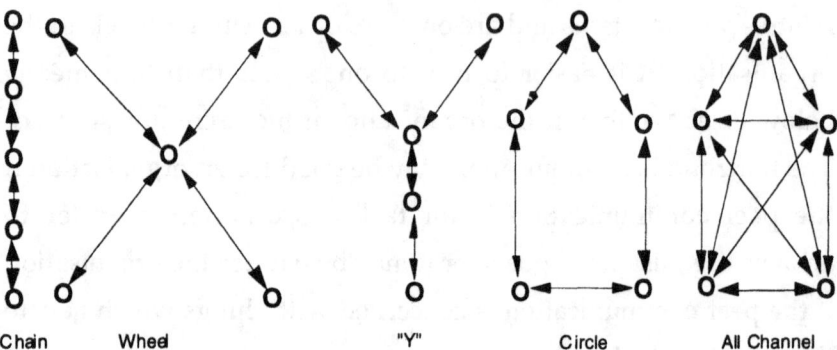

Fig. 11 Communication networks

Chain. In a chain communication network, the communication flows either downwards or upwards in a formally defined chain of command. It is usually found in "tall" organisational hierarchies where communication does not move laterally. For instance, information can flow from the principal, to the deputy principal, to the head of department, to the course coordinator and finally to the class teacher, or vice versa.

Wheel. In a wheel network, communication flows from the subordinates to the centrally placed supervisor, or from the supervisor to the spatially arranged subordinates. In this network, there is no interaction between the subordinates.

"Y" network. In the "Y" network, communication flows from two spatially separated subordinates who report to a supervisor, who in turn reports to his or her superiors. This is the case when the "Y" network is turned upside down. The "Y" network can also represent a kind of communication in which the lower levels have a chain communication linkage, and at the upper level the final supervisor in the chain reports to two superiors who occupy similar levels. The former is the case when faculty deans report to

the principal, and the latter is the case when the principal reports to two deputy vice-chancellors.

Circle. In the circle network, communication is possible between adjoining members only. No interaction takes place between these members and others outside the network. In a circle network the dominant communication type is the horizontal or lateral. All the members in this network appear to be at the same hierarchical level, although they may have a formal leader. This is a typical communication pattern reminiscent of autonomous work groups.

All-channel network. In the all channel network, each member is free to communicate with any other member freely without any restrictions. There is no leader and communication can be initiated from one point to any other point since all members are equal. This is the least structured of all the networks.

The first three networks, chain, wheel and "Y" represent the centralised networks since subordinates report to a supervisor. The circle and the all-channel represent the decentralised networks where there is no formal leader.

All the five networks are important in their own rights depending on the situation under consideration. When solutions to problems and information dissemination are to be achieved fast, the chain, the wheel and the "Y" networks should be preferred so long as the tasks are relatively simple. On the other hand, communication would be much slower in these three networks if the task is complex because the supervisor will be too overloaded with information to make tangible and efficient decisions. When the tasks are complex, then the circle and the all-channel are preferred since they allow interaction between members which enhances richness in decisioin making.

The centralised and the decentralised networks also have a bearing on workers' job satisfaction. In general terms, the centralised networks, that is the chain, the wheel and the "Y", lead to low employees' job satisfaction because workers are not given a chance in decisioin making. Workers in the centralised networks are mainly seen as implementers of decisions which have been made by their superiors. The decentralised networks, that is the circle and the all-channel, yield high job satisfaction since workers' output is recognised in participatory decision making.

The Grapevine

We have, thus far, looked at the formal communication patterns in an organisation. However, the formal communication patterns are just part of a complex communication process taking place in any organisation. The *grapevine* is the informal communication system in an organisation.

Rumours and gossip which pass through the grapevine arise as a result of four main reasons. The first reason is that they help workers to structure and reduce anxiety. Rumours and gossip will continue in an organisation either until the wants and expectations creating the uncertainty underlying the rumour or gossip are fulfiled of until the anxiety is reduced.[13]

The second reason for rumours and gossip is that they help workers try to make sense of limited or disjointed information. Workers strive, through the grapevine, to make sense of information which appears incomplete, and yet very important in their organisation. The third reason is that they help workers to organise themselves into coalitions. The fourth reason is that they make the workers who have "inside" information of the rumours or gossip to have some "power" over whom and how to pass the information.

Grapevine is a very important aspect of organisational communication which managers need to be quite aware of so that the positive aspects of rumours and gossip can be utilised in the management of their organisations, and the negative consequences should be nipped in the bud. Rumours and gossip can be reduced in an organisation by explaining decisions and behaviours in a transparent manner and ensuring that ambiguity is eliminated in organisational communication.

Barriers to Effective Communication

Some of the barriers to effective communication are distortion, filtering, omission, selective perceptions, timeliness and language.

Distortion

Distortion refers to the alteration of the message as it passes from one point to another in the communication channel. Distortion arises as a result of imprecise language, misinterpretation of the message, social distance between the sender and the receiver, and poor choice of symbols and channels. Distortion of a message can also occur by design when people do not want to either hear the message or be party to bad news.

Filtering

Filtering is the process whereby a sender manipulates the information so that it can be received more favourably by the receiver. Sometimes the subordinates filter the information so that their superiors can only know the positive things happening in an organisation. If an organisation has very many hierarchical levels, then the intensity of filtering is quite high.

Omission

Omission occurs when only part of an intended message is passed on to the receiver. People may omit part of a message either because they fear the retributive consequences of their mistakes or because they are unable to grasp the entire message.

Selective perception

Selective perception occurs when receivers selectively see and hear based on their needs, motivations, experience and background and other personal characteristics.[14]

Timeliness

Messages perform the noble task of stimulating action. It is, therefore, important that the transmission of a message be well *timed* in order that appropriate action be taken promptly by the receiver. A lengthy time interval is as bad as a short time interval.

Language

Language is influenced by age, education and the cultural background of both the sender and the receiver. In an educational organisation, as in any other organisation, the teachers, students and other workers come from diverse cultural backgrounds. It is, therefore, imperative that the communication language should take into account the disparities between people or groups in an organisation.

Summary

This chapter begins with an in-depth discussion on communication: its meaning and role, types, networks and barriers. Both the interpersonal and organisational communication have been discussed in detail.

Five communication networks is identified and discussed. These are the chain, wheel, Y, circle and the all-channel. The last part of the chapter discusses six barriers to effective communication. These are distortion, filtering, omission, selective perception, timeliness and language.

END NOTES

[1] F. Luthans, *Organisational Behaviour*, 5th Ed. New York: McGraw-Hill Book Company, 1989, p. 506.

[2] D. Katz and R. Kahn, *The Social Psychology of Organisations*, New York: Wiley, 1978, p. 223.

[3] Aubrey Fischer, *Small Group Decision Making*. New York: McGraw-Hill Book Company, 1974, p. 23.

[4] F. Luthans, *loc. cit.*

[5] S.P. Robbins, *Organisational Behabiour, Concepts and Applications*, 4th Edition. Englewood Cliffs, New Jersey: Prentice Hall, 1989, P. 46..

[6] Ibid, p. 268.

[7] R.M. Steers, *op. cit.* p. 404.

[8] C. Shannon and W. Weaver. *The Mathematical Theory of Communications*. Urbana III: University of Illinois Press, 1948.

[9] S.P. Robbins, *op. cit.* p. 268.

[10] R. Kreitner and A. Kiniki. *Organisational Behaviour*. Homewood, Ill: Irwin, 1989.

[11] E. Hall, *The Silent Language*. New York: Doubleday, 1959.

[12] D. Hellriegel, J.W. Slocum, Jr. and R.W. Woodman. *Organisational Behaviour*, 4th Ed. Minnesotta: West St. Paul, 1986, p. 221.

[13] S.P. Robbins, *op cit.* pp. 280-281.

[14] Ibid, p. 272.

DECISION MAKING

Decision making is defined as the process of specifying the nature of a particular problem and selecting among available alternatives in order to solve it.[1] It is the process of choosing between competing alternatives. This definition of decisioin making indicates that a problem precedes any decision and that there must be a number of alternative courses of action from which an optimum course will be selected.

Making decisions is one of the prime functions of educational management, where decisions are made in such important areas as the allocation of scarce teaching and learning resources, the enrolment of students, employment of teaching and non-teaching staff, the introduction of new curriculum or curriculum reformation, student and staff discipline, staff training and methods of improving pedagogy and educational research. Educational managers need to be conversant with the fundamental processes by which decisions are made in organisations so as to improve teaching and learning effectiveness.

Types of Decisions

There are two types of decisions. These are the *programmed decisions* and the *non-programmed decisions*. Programmed decisions are made on routine problems. In this case the nature of the problem is clearly defined and is well understood by the educational manager. Such programmed decisions in educational organisations include the number of students to be admitted, the promotion of both teaching and non-teaching staff, and disciplining students and staff. The main characteristic of programmed decisions is that the decisioin making process is characterised by high levels of certainty in that the formulation of the problem, its solution phases, rules and procedures are very clearly spelt out.

Non-programmed decisions, on the other hand, are in response to problems which are either novel or poorly defined. For instance, a university chancellor may be faced with such problems as expanding university intake to meet the growing number of students and societal demands and yet university funds are limited, the strengthening of research facilities to increase income from research, or the introduction of fees payment when students have been having free university education. A head teacher may also be faced with such novel problems as buying a school bus when students do not have enough textbooks, increasing the number of students in the school when the boarding and learning facilities are inadequate, and increasing school fees when most parents will be unable to pay. In non-programmed decisions, the educational manager must compare the various alternative courses of action available to him or her and the consequences of these alternatives before an optimum decision is made.

In educational management, leaders at various levels of administrative hierarchy make various decisions in their administrative activities. However, there is a distinct relationship between the administrative level one occupies in the administrative hierarchy and the kind of decisions he or she has to make. Top level educational managers like directors, chancellors and principals are usually faced with non-programmed decisions. On the other hand, deans, departmental heads and other lower level educational managers are usually faced with programmed and routine decisions. This is because non-programmed decisions require leaders with the required conceptual resources to efficiently manage the risks involved in making such decisions. Figure 12 shows this relationship. It is important for educational managers at all levels of decisioin making to recognise the fact that non-programmed decisions are complex and involve a lot of risk-taking, and, therefore, enough time and other resources must be allowed for them. Decisions on new curriculum, expansion of student-enrolment, new fees-structures and the like must not be done in a hurry, or decisions with serious repercussions may be made.

In making non-programmed decisions, the educational manager should be aware of the various risks, uncertainties and costs involved. It is, therefore, imperative that before non-programmed decisions are made, *environmental scanning*, which involves gathering as much information as possible outside the educational organisation, be carefully undertaken. Through environmental scanning an educational manager is capable of acquiring useful information that will help in making a qualitative decision.

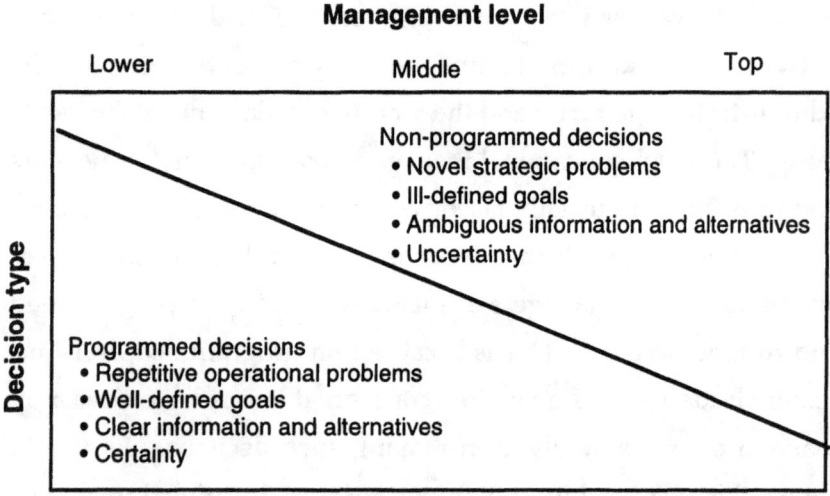

Fig. 12 Relationship of decision type to management level in organisations
Source: R.M. Steers, *Introduction to Organisational Behaviour*, 1991, p. 440.

Three major sets of characteristics are identified in a decisioin making process. The first set refers to those characteristics of the decision maker — how knowledgeable the manager is about the problem; the manager's ability to solve the problem; and his or her level of motivation towards solving the problem. The second set of characteristics refers to the characteristics of the problem itself — is it familiar or unfamiliar, certain or uncertain, complex or simple, stable or unstable. The third set of characteristics refers to the decision's environmental characteristics such as the time required to make the decision, availability of resources, irreversibility of the decision and the significance of the decision.

Individual Decision Making

A number of descriptive models have been designed to describe theoretically and realistically how practising managers make individual decisions.[2] Three models will be discussed in this section. These are (i) econologic or rational or classical; (ii) bounded or administrative; and (iii) the retrospective decisioin making models. It should be noted that these models are also applied in group or participatory decisioin making discussed in the next section.

The econologic (rational or classical) model

The econologic model represents the earliest attempt to formulate a decisioin making model. According to this model the decision maker is perfectly and completely rational in all ways. By being rational it is meant that the decision maker is using the decision strictly as a means to an end. This model assumes that people are economically rational and that they attempt to maximise outcomes in an orderly and sequential process.[3] According to this model, it is assumed that people will select the decision or a course of action which is the most beneficial from among a number of competing alternatives. The model assumes that people search for the most rational decision in a well calculated and systematic fashion. The model has also been referred to as the *economic man model*.

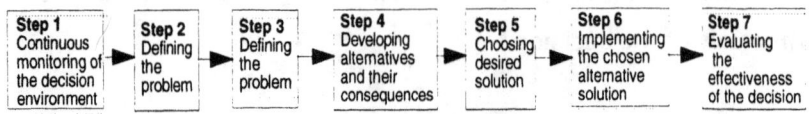

Fig. 13 Steps in the econologic decisioin making process

The econologic model is shown diagrammatically in Figure 13. The first step in this model is the continuous monitoring of the decision environment. In the second step the problems are identified and defined as they arise. In the third step, each problem is analysed to determine its characteristics. After the analysis, alternative solutions are developed in the fourth step. The consequences of each alternative and their costs versus their benefits are also analysed in this step. In step five, the seemingly best or optimum alternative is chosen from among the many alternatives. The chosen alternative decision is implemented in the sixth step. This is followed in step seven by an evaluation of the effectiveness of the decision. Evaluation helps in filling up any gaps or providing a corrective mechanism.

The model assumes that individuals are capable of gathering all the necessary information to enable them make a decision. This is, however, difficult to achieve in organisations. Even the formulation of accurate consequences for the alternatives is difficult to achieve because these consequences lie in the future. The determination of possible alternatives is also very difficult to achieve since not all possible alternatives come to the mind during the decisioin making process: indeed, the best alternatives may be missed out altogether.

The bounded rationality model

The bounded rationality model or the "administrative man model" was presented by Herbert Simon as a more realistic alternative to the econologic model.[4] The basic assumption in this model is that while people seek the best solution, they usually settle for much less because the decisions they confront typically demand greater information processing capabilities than they possess. In other words, people look for a kind of limited (bounded) rationality in decisions.

The bounded rationality concept tries to describe the decisioin making process in three ways: The first way is by using *sequential attention to alternative solutions*. In this case people examine possible solutions to a problem one at a time instead of identifying all possible solutions to the problem, and selecting the best as suggested by the econological model. The various alternatives are identified and evaluated individually. Possible solutions to a problem are tested one after another, the previous one being discarded until an acceptable solution is achieved. The process of looking for alternative solutions stops once an acceptable solution has been found.

The second way is by using *heuristics*. A heuristic is a rule that guides the search for alternatives into areas that have a high probability for yielding satisfactory solutions.[5] The heuristics are used in order to reduce the magnitude of the problem for a speedy decisioin making. Obvious solutions or previous solutions which worked in similar circumstances are analysed and implemented.

The third way is by applying the concept of *satisficing*. In this case, the decision maker, attempts to look for the alternative which is "satisfactory" or "good enough". This way, the bounded rationality model looks at a decision maker as a *satisficer* as opposed to the econologic model which looks at the decision-maker as an *optimiser*.

The decision-makers end up by satisficing because they do not possess the ability to maximise their decisioin making output. This is due to such factors as lack of complete information, shortage of time, costs involved, difficulties in quantifying alternatives and the environmental forces at work.

In the bounded rationality model, the first step is the setting of the goal to be pursued or the definition of the problem to be solved. In the second step, an appropriate level of aspiration is established to determine when a solution is sufficiently positive to be accepted. In the third step, heuristics are employed in order to reduce the various alternatives into a single promising alternative. If no feasible alternative is identified, then the aspiration level is lowered and a new search for alternatives continues. In the fourth step the identified feasible solution is evaluated for its acceptability. If the individual alternative is unacceptable, then the search for a new alternative begins here. In the fifth step if the identified alternative is accepted then it is implemented. In the sixth step, the evaluation of goal attainment takes place for future action.

This decisioin making model is different from the econologic model in the sense that it does not seek the *best* solution, instead it is looking for an *acceptable* solution.

The retrospective decision model

The retrospective decision model deals mainly with non-programmed decisions. It is based on the theory of cognitive dissonance. In this model, the decision maker attempts to rationalise his or her choice on a retrospective basis.

In the first step the *goals* are set. In the second step, an *implicit favourite* (the alternative which is favoured) is identified. In the third step, *implicitly rejected alternatives* are compared and ranked. In the fourth step, a *confirmation* of other *alternative*, which is the second best alternative is made. In the fifth step *decision rule* or *criterion is* established to demonstrate that the *implicit favourite* is superior to the confirmation alternative. In the sixth step, the decision is *announced* and in the seventh step the decision is *implemented*. This decisioin making model is very typical when people want to buy things like cars, clothes or houses. In this model, the individual is convinced that he or she is making a decision in a rational and logical manner.

Participatory (Group) Decision Making

In the previous section we identified three main models in the individual decisioin making process. However, in organistions most decisions should be made through a participatory approach whereby individuals or groups are involved in the decisioin making process. In practical terms, educational managers should be aware that the degree of participation in group decisioin making should be determined by the teachers' experience, education and the nature of the task.

Group or participatory decisioin making process is recommended for a number of reasons. In groups, a lot of knowledge and facts can be gathered very easily since groups have a broader perspective and can collectively consider more alternative solutions. In participatory decisioin making, individuals who participate are usually more satisfied with the decision they have collectively made and they will enthusiastically support it. Participatory decisioin making also helps teachers to communicate freely on matters concerning their profession, and this can be motivating and satisfying.

However, group decisioin making process has some shortcomings. In groups decisions take too long to be made due to long deliberations before a consensus is reached. Sometimes groups are dominated by one individual or a small clique; some decisions become clique decisions and not group decisions. In group decisions, a lot of compromise is involved and this may lead to decisions which are not optimal. In addition, group decisioin making impedes the speed at which some important and urgent decisions can be implemented.

Despite all these negative features of participatory decisioin making, it is very important in decisioin making if maximum output is to be realised from the teachers. What is necessary is a skilful leadership role that attempts to limit the negative impact of group participation. Group participation increases the likelihood that teachers work for rewards and outcomes which they value. It expands the amount of control which teachers have over their own behaviour. Participation in decisioin making is a very useful vehicle for the facilitation of both organisational goal attainment and personal need satisfaction and motivation.

Group or participatory decisioin making utilises consultative and democratic techniques. In consultative techniques the educational manager solicits for subordinates' participation. However, the ultimate decision is in the hands of the superior. In the democractic decisioin making, the whole group deliberates on the problem and through a consensus a decision is made by the entire group.

Normative model of group decision making

The main problem facing managers in a group or participatory decisioin making process is the extent to which they should allow subordinates to participate in making decisions which affect their work. By encouraging participatory decisioin making, managers are in effect decentralising authority within their organisations. This leads to improved decision quality, increased commitments of workers to the decision outcomes which they have influenced, and, above all, it enhances their job satisfaction and motivation.

The normative model of decisioin making was developed by Victor Vroom and Philip Yetton.[6] The Vroom-Yetton model shows how leaders should approach group related decisions. According to this model, there is no leadership style which is appropriate for all situations. It is, therefore, imperative that leaders develop a series of responses which range from autocratic to consultative style and thus apply the leadership style which is most favourable to the decision situation. This model assumes that leaders have to adapt their style to the situation.

The normative model uses *decision effectiveness* to evaluate the effectiveness of a leader. This is done on the basis of three factors, namely, *decision quality* — how important the decisions are for facilitating group performance, *decision acceptance* — how group members accept and implement decisions, and *timeliness* — all decisions must be made in a timely fashion depending on whether they are urgent or not.

The Vroom-Yetton model suggests that leaders should have the skills to apply five decisioin making styles in a continuum from highly autocratic to highly participative.[7] In the first decision style, called *highly autocratic (AI)* the manager can make the decision alone. In the second decision style, which is *less autocratic (AII)*, the manager asks for information from his or her subordinates. However, the decision is made by the manager alone. In the third decision style, the *consultative style (CI)*, the manager shares the problems with the subordinates and asks for their information and evaluation. However, the final decision is made by the manager himself or herself. In the fourth decision style, called the *more consultative* (CII) style, the manager and the subordinates meet as a group to discuss the problem, but the manager makes the decision. In the fifth decision style, called the *highly consultative style (GII).* the manager and subordinates meet as a group to discuss the problem, and the group makes the decision.[8]

Decision Making

It is seen in the preceding paragraphs that this model requires leaders to possess two very important qualities, namely, the ability to make effective decisions and the ability to apply the continuum of the five decision styles depending on the favourableness of the decision situation. The normative model thus provides a decision tree which enables leaders to be effective in decisioin making. In the process of applying the decision tree, leaders answer a series of questions which show, ultimately, the amount of participation to allow the workers so as to maximise decision effectiveness. The model is shown in Figure 14 below.

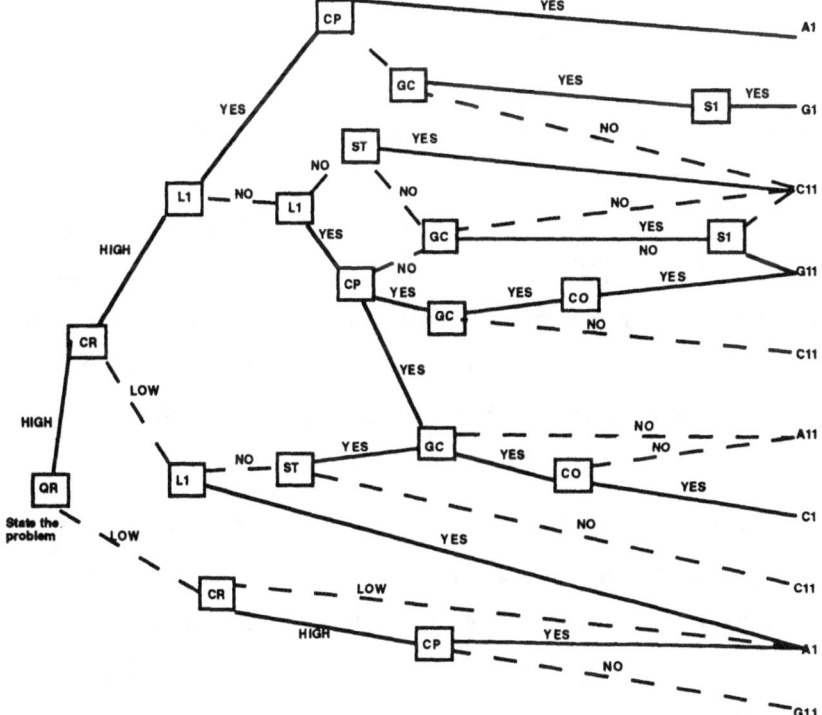

Fig. 14   Decision Making Tree
Source: Adapted from V.H. Vroom, and A.G. Jugo "The new leadership: managing participation in organisations" in R.M. Steers, *Introduction to Organisational Behaviour*, 1991, p. 454.

Abbreviations

(i) QR = Quality requirement - how important is the decision quality?

(ii) CR = Commitment requirement - how important is subordinate commitment?

(iii) LI = Leader's information - how informed and capable is the leader about the problem?

(iv) ST = Problem structure - how structured is the problem?

(v) CP = Commitment probability - how committed would the subordinate be if you made decision alone?

(vi) GC = Goal congruence - how committed are the subordinates in sharing the organisational goals?

(vii) CO = Subordinate conflict - is there likely to be conflict over subordinates' preferred solutions?

(viii) SI = Subordinate information - how informed and capable are the subordinates?

In applying the decision tree, the first question which the leaders ask is the "QR" requirement, followed by "CR" requirement as shown in the figure. The decision maker finally reaches the right hand side of the tree which indicates what decision style should be applied according to the favourableness of the decision situation.

The normative model of decisioin making has important implications in educational management; educational managers are expected to use it as a training device to enable them to see how they would approach different problems by applying the continuum of decision styles.

Groupthink and groupshift: Problems in group decisionmaking

Two by-products of group decisioin making, called *group-think* and *group-shift*, have the potential to affect the group's ability to appraise alternatives objectively and arrive at quality decisioin making.[9]

Groupthink: Group think refers to situations in which group pressures for conformity deter the group from critically appraising unusual, minority or unpopular view.[10] In this phenomenon, group consensus becomes so dominant that it overrides any realistic appraisal of alternative courses of action. The phenomenon was first discussed by Irving Janis and it describes a deterioration in an individual's mental efficiency, reality testing and moral judgements as a result of group pressures.[11]

Some of the symptoms of groups as identified by Janis are:

(i) Group members always have an *illusion of invulnerability* by reassuring themselves and become too optimistic to respond to glaring warning signals.

(ii) Group members always engage in rationalisation by discounting any resistance to the decisions which they have made. They always try to vehemently defend their decisions even in the face of glaring risks.

(iii) Group members always apply a lot of pressure on those members who momentarily express their doubts about the group's shared views or those members who raise questions about the validity of the arguments which support the group decisions.

(iv) Because of group *members' censorship*, those members who may hold differing points of view silently avoid voicing their "dissenting" views by keeping quiet.
(v) Group members always have an illusion of *unanimity* in which members assume that everyone who remains silent is in full agreement with the group decisions. In other words, group members view abstention as a "YES" vote.[12]

As we have seen in the preceding paragraphs groupthink can have several serious deleterious effects on the quality of decisions made by groups. The individuals who may be having important feelings, beliefs and positive critical analysis of decisions are always put under pressure to suppress, withhold or modify them. Because of this, some members are always forced to "appear" to be good members of the group by following the group's decisions even if a different view could have improved the decisions made by groups.

Due to the serious consequences of groupthink the following are some solutions which can help in overcoming these side effects:

(i) Managers or group leaders should encourage individual members to give their own critical evaluations of proposals before a final decision is made. Groups should not be *insulated* by their leaders.
(ii) Managers or group leaders should not state their own positions at the outset, but instead they should promote open inquiry by all members so that a variety of alternatives can be suggested and critically analysed.
(iii) Managers or group leaders may find it more effective to divide groups into two or more subgroups so that

independent views from independent subgroups can be viewed together.

(iv) Managers may invite experts from outside the organisation to challenge members' views at group meetings.

Groupshift: Groupshift refers to a situation where group members, in discussing a given set of alternatives and arriving at a solution, tend to exaggerate the positions which they held earlier. What happens in groups is that a group discussion leads to a significant shift in the positions of members towards a more extreme position in the direction towards which they were already leaning before the discussion.[13]

It has been suggested that as group members discuss freely among themselves, they become more familiar with one another and this makes the members more bold and daring in risk-taking. It is logical to conclude that group membership diffuses individual responsibility and this exonerates each member from the dire consequences of the decisions made by the groups and, therefore, members become more brave in risk-taking during decisioin making.

The Problem-solving Process as a Cycle of Events

A problem is an issue which requires a solution. Problem-solving is thus a technique in decisioin making. The outcome of a problem is a decision. An issue becomes a problem when it reaches a level which is difficult to reasonably tolerate. This is the condition when the school environment moves from placid to turbulent.[14] In other words, a problem is recognised when there is a performance gap.

The problem-solving cycle is divided into five main stages as identified at Elmwood High.[15] These are:

(a) The problem recognition stage.
(b) The problem screening stage.
(c) The buffer penetrating stage.
(d) Distribution of the problem to the various centres.
(e) Implementation and feedback.

The problem recognition stage

The first stage in the problem solving cycle is concerned with the recognition of the problem. As has been indicated earlier, a problem occurs when there is a performance gap. It is thus imperative that an educational manager should recognise and define the problem so that it becomes well understood by those who are concerned with its solution.

The problem screening stage

The problem screening stage, or the buffering out stage, is concerned with putting the problem in its proper perspective. It is a question of determining the magnitude of the problem by passing it through a selective device. The problem screening stage is divided into five sub-stages. These are:

(i) *No jurisdiction.* This is the first buffer which applies the "clean hand principle." In this case the educational manager declines to solve the problem since he or she has no authority to do so. This is the case when the problem can be best solved by, say, the ministry of education, the police, the ministry of lands or the board governing the school. It is imperative that the educational manager carefully determines where the problem belongs so that efficiency and effectiveness in problem solution are enhanced.

(ii) *Strategic catharsis.* This is the second buffer which applies the "letting off steam principle". In this strategy the complainant is allowed to talk his or her problem out. If you allow someone to "talk out" his or her complaint then the problem becomes smaller in magnitude.

(iii) *Strategic stalling.* This is the third buffer which applies the "natural death principle". In this case an educational manager either consciously or unconsciously assigns such a very low priority to a problem that it is never acted upon. Educational managers should be very careful in choosing the problems which can be allowed to die their natural death without jeopardising the entire organisational set-up.

(iv) *Strategic ignoring.* This is the fourth buffer which applies the "innocent until proved guilty principle". It is important at times to let problems lie dormant with the hope that they will be forgotten.

(v) *Mutual reinforcement.* This is the fifth buffer which applies the "safe ground principle". In this case, teachers speak with "one voice" to defend their profession or decision. It helps in enhancing group, rather than individual, accountability which provides a protective shield to individual group members.

Buffer penetrating stage

The buffer can be removed in two ways. The first method of removing the buffer is when an educational manager, together with his or her management team, willingly decide to solve a specific problem. The second method is when the buffer is penetrated forcefully by internal and external pressures, requiring school personnel to tackle a problem which they would otherwise overlook.[16]

There are five major patterns, which have been identified, that cause the buffer to be penetrated.[17] These are:

(i) *Intermittent renewal pattern.* This is when the tension surrounding an issue or a problem refuses to die and repeatedly arises seeking further attention. When further attention is provided then the buffer has been penetrated and the problem solving cycle is once again started.

(ii) *Crisis management.* This is the case when teachers, students, parents or an entire society raise such noise about an issue that it cannot just be ignored by the educational management. The crisis may be in the form of a sit-in, demonstration or a serious strike.

(iii) *Central office-directives.* This happens when the aggrieved parties petition higher authorities responsible for educational policies. Such petitions trigger off commands or directives from the hierarchy that the educational manager can no longer ignore. The buffer is thus penetrated.

(iv) *Identifying the "soft spot".* In this case the aggrieved party looks for an "area of weakness" or the "compliant part" of the management which can both listen and successfully solve the problem. It is important to find out the permeable part of the decisioin making machinery.

(v) *Voluntary removal of the buffer.* This is when the educational management voluntarily decides to solve the problem since it is in the best interest of the organisation to do so. The voluntary removal of the buffer leads to the fourth stage.

Distribution of the problem to the various centres

When the problem has penetrated the buffer and its solution unanimously agreed upon then it is distributed to the appropriate sphere of influence or an area within whose jurisdiction it falls. It is important to have decisional jurisdictions[18] which have been established on the basis of expertise.

The distribution of problems to the relevant spheres of influence is a very essential part of delegation of authority and helps an organisation to deal with dissimilar problems simultaneously. This enhances the efficiency of management.

Implementation and feedback

When an appropriate decisional jurisdiction has carefully considered the problem and a decision has been made, then the decision is implemented. Implementation of the decision is followed by evaluation, and through a proper feedback mechanism all the interested parties are informed of the success or failure of the decisional process.

Techniques of Improving Decision Making

In the preceding sections we have, thus far, considered both individual and group (participatory) decisioin making. A number of decisioin making models at both individual and group levels have been presented and elucidated. It is important for an educational manager to first of all identify the problem and find out whether it should be solved individually by himself or by any other member (individual decisioin making) or whether it should be solved by a given group (group or participatory decisioin making). It is impractical to provide an ideal framework for decisioin making in educational settings. However, the preceding sections have made serious attempts at exposing the educational manager to a variety of decisioin making models which will hopefully shape the decisioin making skill and speed of managers in educational organisations.

This section discusses three group decisioin making techniques which educational managers can apply in order to improve the decisioin making effectiveness and efficiency in their organisations. The three techniques are brainstorming, nominal group and the Delphi techniques. These techniques help in reducing the inter-group interactions of groupthink and groupshift.

Brainstorming

This technique involves an educational manager or group leader asking his or her staff members to come together, and they are given a specific problem to solve. The teachers or relevant staff members are then asked to freely give their suggestions and alternative solutions to the problem. In the early stages of brainstorming, the group leader ensures that criticisms are minimised so that free expressions by the teachers are not inhibited. All the proposals and alternative solutions are recorded in detail.

After all the ideas have been recorded then the educational manager helps the teachers in considering the positive and negative aspects of each teacher's proposal. With proper guidance, and objective analysis of the various alternatives the brainstorming session should be able to help teachers come up with the best solution to the problem under the circumstances. Brainstorming helps in stimulating group members to offer their "best" ideas for improving group decisions.

Nominal group technique (NGT)

NGT consists of four phases in the group decisioin making process.[19] The first phase consists of individual members meeting as a group. However, they sit silently and independently generating their own ideas on a problem which has already been presented to them. In the second phase, a round-robin procedure ensues whereby each group member presents his or her ideas to the group without any discussion. All these ideas are summarised and recorded carefully by the "group leader". In the third phase, all the ideas generated are discussed for clarification and evaluation by the group members. In the fourth phase, all the group members silently and individually give their rank-ordering of the various solutions to the problem. The final decision of the group is determined mathematically by the pooled outcome of the members' votes on the issue.[20] The idea with the highest aggregate ranking determines the eventual group decision.

A review of existing literature indicates that NGT-led groups come up with many more ideas than traditional interacting groups.[21] The main reason is that every member independently considers the problem at issue without influence from other group members.

Delphi technique

The Delphi technique was named after the oracle at Delphi in ancient Greece.[22] The Delphi technique maintains anonymity amongst members; members are never allowed to meet face to face. The technique applies the following steps:

(i) After the identification of a problem, a panel of members, usually experts, is formed. The members are never allowed to come face to face.

(ii) The members are then asked, through a series of carefully designed questionnaires, to suggest potential solutions to the problem.

(iii) The results of the questionnaire are then circulated among all the group members, after compilation at a central location.

(iv) When the members have viewed the feedback, they are then asked about their opinions, in order to find out if the opinions of the others in the first questionnaire changed their mind. This process is repeated until group members' opinions begin to show evidence of a consensus on the problem's solution.

One of the advantages of the Delphi technique is that it insulates the group members from the interactional influence. It also allows the panel of experts to benefit from the estimates of others. However, this technique is quite time consuming and costly. Where speedy decisions are to be made, the Delphi technique is not appropriate. In addition the technique does not provide for the development of a rich array of alternatives.

Deciding and Doing

Decisions made in an educational organisation should be put to effect if the resources mobilised during the decisioin making processes are not to be wasted. Herbert Simon stresses that the task of "deciding" pervades the entire administrative organisation quite as much as does the task of "doing"[23]. In an effective educational management, the process of deciding should be intimately succeeded by the process of doing. A decision becomes useful for an organisation only when it has been implemented, otherwise it still remains "a good intention".

It is thus imperative that when teachers have been called upon to mobilise their resourcefulness for both determining appropriate decisions and methods for ensuring conclusive action they are eventually convinced that their energies were not in vain. Teachers derive a lot of satisfaction and motivation when they see their professional efforts being put into use in determining the course of their organisation. Decision making is simply a means to an end, the end being the impact of the decision on the organisation. An effective educational management provides an incisive mechanism for both correct decisioin making and effective action.

Summary

This chapter deals with decisioin making. Both the individual and group decisioin making types are discussed in detail. The econologic, bounded rationality and the retrospective models are discussed under the individual decisioin making type. On the group decisioin making type the normative model isdiscussed in detail. The groupthink and groupshift is also discussed here.

The problem-solving process as a cycle of events isdiscussed in the next part of the Chapter. The five stages in the problem solving cycle are analysed in detail. The techniques for improving decisioin making in educational management are also discussed. The chapter has ended by emphasising that the task of "deciding" is as much important as the task of "doing" in any educational organisation for effective management.

END NOTES

[1] K. Mackrimon and R. Taylor, "Decision making and problem solving", in M.D. Dunnette, (ed.), *Handbook of Industrial and Organisational Psychology*. Chicago: Rand and McNally, 1976, pp. 1397-1453.

[2] F. Luthans, *Organisational Behaviour*, 5th Ed. New York: McGraw-Hill Book Company, 1989, p. 535.

[3] R.M. Steers, *Introduction to Organisational Behaviour*, 4th Ed. New York: Harper Collins Publishers, Inc., 1991, p. 442.

[4] H.A. Simon, *Administrative Behaviour: A Study of Decision Making Process in Administrative Organisations*. 3rd Ed. New York: Free Press, 1976, pp. 61-78.

[5] R.M. Steers, *loc. cit.*

[6] V. Vroom and P. Yetton, *Leadership and Decision Making*. University of Pittsburgh Press, 1973.

[7] R.M. Steers, p. 452.

[8] Ibid. pp. 452-453.

[9] S.P. Robbins, *Organisational Behaviour: Concepts, Controversies and Applications*. New Jersey, Englewood Cliffs: Prentice Hall, 1989, p. 287.

[10] Ibid.

[11] I.L. Janis, *Victims of Groupthink*. Boston: Houghton Mifflin, 1972.

[12] Ibid.

[13] S.P. Robbins, *op. cit.* p. 288.

[14] F.E. Emery, and E.L. Trist, "The causal texture of organisation environment", in *Human Relations* 18, 1965.

[15] E.M. Hanson, *Educational Administration and Organisational Behaviour*. Boston: Allyn and Bacon, Inc., 1979, p. 368.

[16]Ibid. p. 370.

[17]Ibid, pp. 371-372.

[18]N. Brown, "A contingency approach to educational decision making: A case study of governance in the high school", in Hanson, E.M. *op. cit.* p. 372.

[19]A.H. Van DenVan, and A. Delbecq, "The effectiveness of nominal, delphi, and interacting group decision making processes", in *Academy of Management Journal* 17, 1974, 607-626.

[20]R.M. Steers, *op. cit.* p. 466.

[21]A.H. Van DenVan, *Group Decision Making Effectiveness.* Kent, Ohio: Kent State University Centre for Business and Economic Research Press, 1974.

[22]F. Luthans, *op. cit.* p. 544.

[23]A. Simon, *Administrative Behaviour: A Study of Decision Making Process in Administrative Organisations.* 3rd Ed. New York: Free Press, 1976, p. 1.

SUPERVISION: GENERAL AND INSTRUCTIONAL

A Historical Perspective

In order to understand the modern supervisory techniques better, it is appropriate to trace supervisory trends from the earlier American education systems.

In America, a statute was adapted in 1654 that empowered selectmen of towns to be responsible for appointing teachers of sound faith and morals.[1] The appointed teachers would only stay in office as long as they possessed these stipulated qualities. During this period of *"administrative inspection"* (1642-1875) supervision was handled by laymen who included the clergy, school wardens, trustees, selectmen and citizens' committees.

Supervision concentrated on such matters as appraising the general achievement of pupils in subject matter, evaluating methods used by teachers, observing the general management of schools and conduct of pupils and ascertaining whether money spent on education was wisely expended.

These early supervisory concepts were characterised by inspection. When an educator became the supervisor or the director of instruction, he was called the inspector.[2] The functions of the inspector were more judicial than executive in nature.

The supervisor or inspector made judgement about the teacher rather than the teaching or the pupil's learning in the classroom. Supervisors made their decisions on the basis of what they saw. An analysis of these supervisory techniques shows that supervision during this period was mainly concerned with the management of schools and the fulfilment of the prescribed curricular needs rather than the improvement of teaching and learning.

During the period that followed, *efficiency orientation* (1876-1936), attention was now being placed on assisting the teachers to improve their teaching effectiveness.[3] It was during this period that educational professionals replaced the lay people in supervisory activities. The supervisors started providing a friendly atmosphere and a warm interpersonal relationship for the supervised teachers.

The autocratic relationships between the supervisors and the teachers began to wane during the succeeding period. This gave rise to the period of *co-operative group effort* (1937-1959). As towns grew in size and the general population increased in numbers, there was need for supervision of instruction. This was mainly because of the shortage of qualified teachers which necessitated the employment of a large number of untrained teachers. This is the period which marked the establishment of the posts of *superintendent of schools* and *special-area supervisors*. The superintendent of schools was the chief executive of the school system and the special-area supervisors were in charge of the special subjects which were being introduced in the curriculum. The increase in the total number of positions in general, and special-area supervision, in the school system made cooperation and coordination essential.

The foregoing period was followed by the current period of *research orientation* (1960 to present). School administration and supervision are being studied with increasingly improved research procedures and professionally inspired vigour.[4]

Definition

Supervision is today considered as that dimension or phase of educational administration which is concerned with improving instructional effectiveness. Both the definitions of supervision and administration show the validity of the idea that supervision is an integral part of administration.

Supervision evolved from the realisation that we accomplish very little alone, and that we cannot accomplish much by simply grouping people together. For any kind of group to hold together, there must first of all be a common objective that the members of the group are committed to. Secondly, a direction is needed to channel the diverse and often disorganised efforts of the individuals into a purposeful stream of productivity to achieve the common objective. Thirdly, newer and better supervisory techniques must be developed through research effort and applied in order to release the maximum potentials of the teachers.

Supervision can be divided into *general supervision* and *instructional supervision*. General supervision subsumes supervisory activities that take place principally outside the classroom. Such activities include the writing and revision of curricula, preparation of units and materials of instruction, the development of processes and instruments for reporting to parents and such broad concerns as the evaluation of the total educational programme. Instructional supervision on the other hand is concerned with the pupil or the student learning in the classroom.

The most recent concept in instructional supervision is called *clinical supervision*. Clinical supervision is the rationale and practice designed to improve the teacher's classroom performance. Its principal data are obtained from the events which take place in the classroom. The analysis of these data and the relationship between the teacher and the supervisor form the basis of the programme, procedures and strategies designed to improve the students' learning by improving the teachers' learning behaviour constitute clinical supervision.[5]

Goldhammer et al. have defined clinical supervision as that phase of instructional supervision which draws its data from first-hand observation of actual teaching events, and involves face to face (and other associated interactions) interaction between the supervisor and the teacher in the analysis of teaching behaviours and activities for instructional improvement.[6]

From the foregoing definition, the role of a supervisor encompasses *administrative, curricular* and *instructional* dimensions. The *administrative dimension* includes:
(i) setting and prioritising goals.
(ii) providing long range planning.
(iii) designing organisational structures between persons and groups.
(iv) organising and securing resources.
(v) selection of teaching staff.
(Vi orientation of new staff.
(vii) promoting the school community relations.
(viii) establishing both academic and disciplinary standards.

The *curricular dimension* includes:
(i) developing curricular programmes and changes.
(ii) selecting materials and allocating resources.
(iii) estimating the expenditure needs for the curriculum.
(iv) assisting regular staff in upgrading their curricular capacities.
(v) informing the public about the school's curricular activities and innovations.
(vi) relating the curricular activities to the community resources.

The *instructional dimension* includes:
(i) helping in the formulation and implementation of schemes of work.
(ii) evaluating the instructional programmes and overseeing modifications.
(iii) delivering instructional resources.
(iv) helping in conducting and coordinating staff in-servicing.

(v) advising and assisting teachers involved in instructional programmes.
(vi) procuring funds required for instructional purposes.
(vii) receiving community feedback about school programmes.

Supervisory Activities

Supervision is an administrative activity whose strategy is to stimulate teachers towards greater pedagogic effectiveness and productivity. It is a means towards an end but not an end in itself. Supervision must not be confused with "inspection" or "snoopervision" which have autocratic connotations for compliance.

In this section the major supervisory activities are discussed within the framework of selected administrative processes.

Planning

Supervisors must allocate time for planning in sufficient details to satisfy the requirements of their teachers. The foremost task of a supervisor is, therefore, to identify the objectives of the educational organisation or school and the means by which they can be achieved. A supervisor helps in the initiation of action for the achievement of individual or group goals. Supervisory behaviour is primarily concerned with improving the setting for teaching and learning. Supervisors are thus concerned with the development and accomplishment of educational goals by working with and through the teachers.

Supervisors should be expert educational programme leaders and because of this expectation their work should reflect a high value for administrative, curricular and instructional enhancement. It is not in doubt that educational institutions have been established to achieve specific goals desired by the society, but not to guarantee employment to individual teachers or workers. Therefore, supervisory leadership must play a leading role in the attainment of the pre-determined goals by improving the quality of management, curriculum and instruction.

Organising

Supervisory leadership helps in the division of work and assignment of duties for the achievement of the educational objectives. It is the obligation of supervisors to train and develop their teachers and other subordinates so that the constantly recurring departmental problems can be solved efficiently and effectively. In this regard, supervisors must free themselves from unnecessary burdens of detail by delegating some duties as well as authority to make decisions to subordinates capable of handling them. Supervisory leadership is important in the selection and assignment of teachers and other subordinates for the enhancement of teaching and learning.

Coordination

Supervisory behaviour ascertains that all parts of an educational organisation are maintained and interrelated for a harmonious operation in order that the objectives are achieved smoothly. Supervisors must, therefore, strive to promote an effective working relationship within all the departments of the entire educational organisation.

An effective supervisory leadership must develop an articulated and co-ordinated programme of study throughout the entire educational organisation.

Influencing

Gregg introduced *influencing* as an administrative process to replace such authoritative concepts as commanding, directing and controlling.[7] Influencing denotes an attempt to motivate teachers, students and other personnel concerned with education. The supervisor should have the ability to exercise human relations approach in dealing with teachers and students. He should be able to initiate action, portray exemplary behaviour in leadership and constantly seek the opinion of his or her subordinates.

In order that the supervisors become effective in influencing their subordinate's they must be conversant with the various theories of work motivation and job satisfaction discussed in Chapter Three. Supervisors must recognise their important role as *change agents*. This suggests that the effective supervisor must be aware of promising developments, sense how a social invention can be adapted to his or her particular school, and develop a series of appropriate strategies for disseminating promising and imaginative curricular and instructional practices within the educational organisation.[8]

Communicating

For effective supervisory leadership, supervisors should be able to communicate their ideas and intentions to the teachers clearly and precisely. Communication enables supervisors to transmit and accurately replicate ideas, ensured by a proper feedback mechanism, for the purpose of eliciting actions which will accomplish the goals of an educational organisation. Supervisors spend a large portion of their time talking to colleagues, dictating letters, participating in meetings, consulting with parents and other community members, preparing reports and so on.

Staff relations are influenced by communication. Teachers and other staff members want to express to the supervisors their opinions about job assignments, working conditions, and other matters relating to their interests in curriculum and instruction. A two-way communication system is, therefore, necessary for both the supervisors and the supervised for exchange of opinions in order to enhance instructional effectiveness.

Evaluation

Supervisory leadership is an on-going activity which begins with the orientation and induction of new teachers in order to assimilate them into the educational organisation. It enables teachers to gain an understanding of the latest trends and developments in education and teaching through purposefully designed in-service and out-of-service training and development programmes. Supervisory leadership also helps teachers to develop syllabi, curriculum guides, purposeful units of instruction and lesson plans. Having ascertained that all the resources, both human and material, are appropriately procured and provided within an enabling environment for maximum utilisation, it is then incumbent upon supervisors to ascertain how well the assigned responsibilities are being undertaken to achieve the organisational objectives.

Evaluation thus enables the supervisors to make decisions which will enable the educational process within an organisation to be improved for an effective achievement of the predetermined objectives. A supervisory programme is incomplete if it does not have an evaluation report. In this case a supervisor acts as an *educational auditor* whose function is to verify the teaching and learning outcomes in order to provide a corrective mechanism.

From the foregoing discussion on supervisory activities, it is evident that supervision is an important strategy for stimulating teachers towards greater pedagogic effectiveness so that an educational organisation functions efficiently in meeting the societal objectives. Supervision is thus an administrative activity which has an important coordinating and influencing device. Supervision should, in this regard, be viewed as the administrative oil that lubricates the management engine.

Basic Skills in Supervision

In order to provide an effective supervisory leadership supervisors must acquire basic skills. These basic skills include conceptual, human relations and technical skills.

Conceptual skills

Conceptual skills involve the ability to acquire, analyse and interpret information in a logical manner. Supervisors must understand both the internal and external environments in which

Supervision: General and Instructional 183

they operate. They also need to understand the effects of the changes in one or more of those environments on the organisation for which they work.

It is imperative that supervisors should enhance their supervisory effectiveness by acquiring newer and emerging concepts and techniques in supervision. Through further training and staff seminars the conceptual capacities of supervisors can be expanded.

Human relations skills

The human relations skills refer to the ability to understand the teachers and to interact effectively with them. Human relations skills enable the supervisors to act both officially and humanely. A supervisor should, therefore, be able to efficiently link both the organisational and individual goals so that teachers can be *milked dry* of their professional potentials.

The human relations skills are important for dealing with teachers not only as individuals but also as groups. The human relations skills can be acquired from both training and experience.

Technical skills

Technical skills include understanding and being able to perform effectively the specific processes, practices and techniques required of specific jobs in an organisation. Although the supervisors may not be expected to have all the technical answers, they need an overall knowledge of the functions they supervise and sources of specific information. While the supervisors can seek advice from specialists, they need to have enough technical knowledge in order to make sound judgements.

Supervisory Skills and Management Levels

Figure 15 shows the application of skills in supervision according to management levels, for effective supervision. More conceptual and less technical skills are needed as one advances from the lower to the higher management levels in an educational organisation. Supervisors or administrators at the lower management levels need considerable technical skills because they are often required to train and develop technicians and other employees in their areas of jurisdiction or departmnts. On the other hand, top managers or supervisors in educational organisations only need to be conversant with how tasks are performed at the operational level.

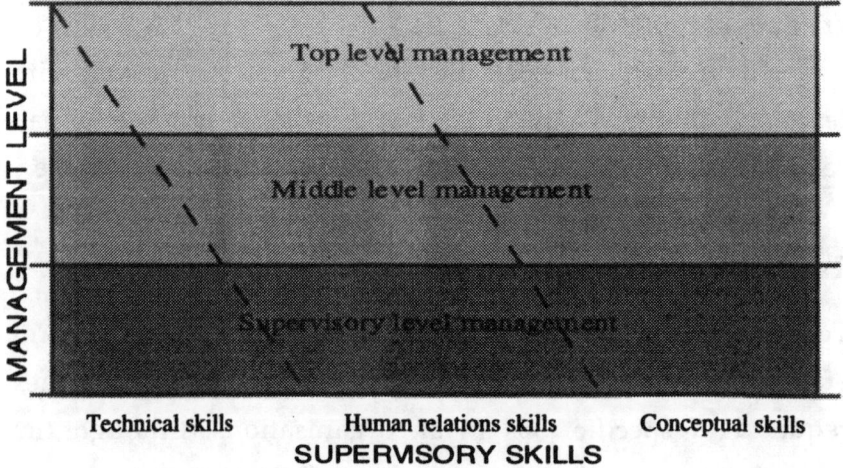

Figure 15. Supervisory skills and management levels

However, the common denominator, that is the skills that are very crucial and are universally required at all management levels, are the human relations skills. This is because the way employees relate to one another in an organisation must be seen to be humane at all times and at all management levels. The human relations skills thus universally transcend all management levels.

Instructional Supervision in Practice: The Supervisory Aspect of Teaching Practice

The most ideal application of instructional supervision is during teaching practice. Teaching practice is a very important activity which is undertaken by all teacher trainees in the course of their training. It affords the teacher trainees an opportunity to apply their learned professional and academic skills in a practical learning and teaching environment. During teaching practice, teacher trainees are exposed to all aspects of the school environment and it is, therefore, the beginning of practical professionalisation.

The Instructional Supervisor

The teacher, tutor or lecturer who is charged with the responsibility of supervising a teacher trainee during teaching practice is called an instructional supervisor. The instructional supervisor, from the educational management point of view, must be conversant with the basic techniques of instructional supervisory leadership. He or she must have prior exposure to the various supervisory activities. A serious attempt must also be undertaken by the educational management to provide the instructional supervisors with the opportunity to acquire and practise the important skills required in supervision. Of course it is expected that the instructional supervisor is a professionally qualified teacher, with the pedagogical skills at his or her finger tips.

Although the instructional supervisor is an expert in pedagogy, having acquired this through both theoretical and practical exposure, his or her instructional supervisory leadership skills must be consciously developed through training. This is because courses on instructional supervision at the university are offered to very few education students.

The Instructional Supervision Process

The instructional supervision process is a well-planned and progressive one which starts outside the classroom before the actual classroom teaching and ends outside the classroom after the observation of an actual classroom teaching. This is a systematic process with a well-defined beginning and ending. For clarity, the institutional supervision process during teaching practice is divided into three main phases in this book.

(i) The pre-observation conference;
(ii) The observation conference;
(iii) The post-observation conference.

The pre-observation conference

The pre-observation conference phase refers to the period that precedes the actual classroom teaching observation. It is the period during which the instructional supervisor strives to develop a rapport between himself and the teacher trainee. This is the most important phase in instructional supervision since what transpires during this period has a very significant bearing on the success or failure of the entire instructional supervisory leadership. The way the instructional supervisor eases the teacher trainee in order to provide an enabling supervisory environment for both himself and the teacher trainee is the foremost task in instructional supervisory leadership. The pre-observation conference may start with a cordial greeting between the two, and proceed with rather general discussion, not necessarily relevant to the lesson to be observed.

Having performed the above preliminaries, the instructional supervisor then obtains from the teacher trainee the requisite documents which include a lesson plan, scheme of work, record of work and a class file. The foremost function of this phase is to provide a conducive environment within which the instructional supervisory leadership takes place in order to release maximum potentials from both the teacher trainee and the instructional supervisor. This phase of instructional supervision could be conducted in the staff-room or any other place which has been allocated by the school for this purpose. If time does not allow, then the instructional supervisor and the teacher trainee can conduct this phase as they both walk towards the class in which the lesson is to be observed. It is important for the instructional supervisor to refer to the teacher trainee by name.

The observation conference

The observation conference begins when the teacher trainee and the instructional supervisor enter the classroom. It is preferred that the instructional supervisor be introduced to the class by the teacher trainee after greetings have been exchanged with the class.

The instructional supervisor then sits at the back of the classroom. As the lesson proceeds, he or she makes anecdotal notes of how both teaching and learning go on during the period. The supervisor must follow the lesson in detail from the beginning to the end. This phase of instructional supervision calls for the pedagogic skills of the instructional supervisor.

During this phase the instructional supervisor records the teacher trainee's performance on the format of the lesson plan, the appropriateness of the lesson objectives, the integration of lecturing and other relevant pedagogic methods, reinforcement, stimulus variation, personality and confidence of the teacher trainee, classroom discipline, chalkboard use, consistency in teaching to the objectives and the ability of teacher trainee to provide an appropriate feedback mechanism. The instructional supervisor must be cognisant of the fact that his or her presence in the class should have a minimal influence on the entire classroom behaviour. Of course, the presence of an instructional supervisor will have some influence on the entire classroom behaviour and, therefore, one of his or her major tasks during this phase is to minimise it as much as possible. This can be achieved by ensuring that the taking of the anecdotal notes does not give the teacher trainee or the students a clue as to when a favourable or unfavourable remark is being recorded. The facial expression should also not indicate approval or disapproval. The main idea is to create for the teacher trainee, the students and the instructional supervisor an "intimidation-free" teaching-learning-supervision environment.

The anecdotal notes taken during this phase should give details about the teacher trainee's pedagogic strengths and weaknesses.

Post-observation conference

This is the final phase of the instructional supervision programme. This phase must be conducted in *privacy*. A school should be able to provide the instructional supervisor and the teacher trainee with a private office or place which enables them to discuss the progress of the observed lesson freely and fairly. It is true that some instructional supervisors may be tempted to conduct this phase in a staff room or in a place that does not provide the privacy that this important professional exercise deserves. This negates the very essence of an effective instructional supervision and must be avoided at all costs. True, some schools may be incapable of providing an ideal place for this phase. However, it is incumbent upon the instructional supervisor, in such a situation, to look for an appropriate alternative which provides the environment required for this exercise.

When an appropriate place has been identified, the instructional supervisor should further provide a rapport between himself and the teacher trainee. This could be initiated by asking the teacher trainee how he or she "found the lesson today". As the discussion progresses, the instructional supervisor informs the teacher trainee of his or her strengths as were detected during the lesson, before the weaknesses can be exposed. This order is very important for motivation purposes.

During the post-observation conference, the instructional supervisor must apply democratic techniques as much as possible. The instructional supervision process is a great learning opportunity not only for the teacher trainee but also for the instructional supervisor. Under such circumstances the teacher trainee may be able to convince the instructional supervisor why he or she thinks the application of a given teaching method during the lesson was more appropriate than the other. An effective instructional supervisor is one who recognises the fact that learning is a two-way process and that supervisory leadership meets the purported objective if an enabling environment is provided for the maximum release of the potentials of the teacher trainee. The feedback during the post-observation conference should be seen by both the instructional supervisor and the teacher trainee in terms of shared information. The incorporation of valid suggestions of the teacher trainee in the supervisory feedback helps to build his or her confidence. This enhances the learning process.

The instructional supervisor should recognise and emphasise alternative approaches to teaching. Application of a variety of skills should not only be encouraged, but should also be recognised in order to strengthen the teacher trainee's pedagogic skills.

The feedback during the post-observation conference should focus on modifiable teaching behaviours. An effective post-observation conference recognises the limitations of the teaching and learning environment. Teacher trainees should not be asked to do things which they cannot do anything about. In other words, the post-observation conference must provide realistic possibilities for problem-solving. For instance, a supervisory feedback which requires the teacher trainee to improve on his or her naturally croaking voice, or to write high up the chalkboard when he or she is actually too short for this, or to avail a teaching aid which the school cannot afford, miserably fails to be sensitive to the teaching-learning environment.

The teaching process is systematic and is deliberately planned to proceed the way it is during a given lesson so that maximum learning is realised. It is, therefore, incumbent upon the instructional supervisor to focus on specific and concrete teaching behaviours as they were noticed during the classroom observation. The feedback session during the post-observation conference should thus discuss specific, but not general, issues so that the teacher trainee can maximise the benefits of instructional supervision during this phase. In the same token this feedback session should be conducted in a descriptive rather than an evaluative manner. The feedback session should be seen by both the instructional supervisor and the teacher trainee as a supportive activity which aims at strengthening the teacher trainee's confidence by improving on his or her strengths and providing opportunities for learning more techniques.

The issues discussed during the post-observation conference should be timed in such a manner that the teacher trainee is provided with an immediate feedback. A feedback session is effective if it focuses on the present rather than the past. However, the feedback should not be made immediate at the expense of its objectivity. The instructional supervisor should, therefore, strive to provide both an immediate and an objective feedback devoid of subjectivity.

The post-observation conference should end with a well thought-out summary of the discussion in order to enable the teacher trainee to remember the key issues discussed during this exercise. An effective instructional supervisory leadership should insist on building upon previous discussions so as to allow the teacher trainee to consistently develop the pedagogic skills throughout the teaching practice session. It is recommended that if time allows, the instructional supervisor should talk to the assisting teacher or head-teacher so as to have an inkling about the overall behaviour of the teacher trainee.

Supervision and Inspection

A clear distinction should be made between supervision and inspection. As has already been seen, supervision is a more recent concept in management which developed as a result of the need to work with and through people in a more humane understanding. Inspection, on the other hand, is an old concept in management whose basic precept is that of autocratic management which is aimed at catching the workers red-handed. This is a fault-finding attitude in management.

In management, supervision and inspection are not synonymous. This is because the processes have different objectives and occur at different stages in the management task. Supervision is an on-going activity in management between a subordinate and a superordinate and provides a common understanding between them. Inspection, on the other hand, is a one-time fact-finding activity.

Summary

This chapter begins with a historical perspective on supervision as applied in educational management. This part shows how supervision has evolved from a totally autocratic approach in the past to democratic participation at the moment. The operating definition of instructional supervision is provided, which shows that it is an integral part of educational management. The general supervision and instructional supervision are distinguished. Three dimensions, namely: administrative, curricular and instructional are identified as important dimensions of supervision in educational management.

In the next part of the chapter the supervisory activities of planning, organising, coordinating, influencing, communicating and evaluating have been analysed. The **three basic skills**, namely: conceptual, human relations and technical **are also been** discussed. This is followed by a detailed **application of** instructional supervision during teaching practice. **The teaching** practice supervision is divided into **three main phases: the** pre-observation conference; the observation conference; and, the post-observation conference. The final part of the Chapter provides a distinction between supervision and inspection.

END NOTES

[1] G.G. Eye and L.A. Netzer, *Supervision of Instruction: A Phase of Administration*. New York: Harper and Row Publishers, 1965, p. 5.

[2] Ibid.

[3] Ibid. p. 9

[4] Ibid.

[5] L.M. Cogan, *Clinical Supervision*. Boston: Houghton Mifflin Company, 1973, pp. 8-9.

[6] R. Goldhammer, R.H. Anderson and R.J. Krajewski, *Clinical Supervision: Special Methods for the Supervision of Teachers*. New York: Holt, Rinehart and Winston Inc., 1980, pp. 19-20.

[7] R.T. Gregg, "The administrative process," in R.F. Campbell and R.T. Gregg, (eds.) *Administrative Behaviour in Education*. New York: Harper and Row, 1957, p. 254.

[8] S.J. Knezevich, *Administration of Public Education*. New York: Harper and Row, Publishers, 1975, p. 372.

Chapter Nine

FINANCIAL MANAGEMENT IN EDUCATION

An Overview

Financial management in education is concerned with the cost of education, sources of income to meet the educational costs and the spending of the income in an objective manner in order to achieve the educational objectives.

Education is both a consumption and an investment in human capital by individuals and society. Educated people acquire knowledge, skills and attitudes which enable them to receive higher earnings and also to play an active role in societal development. These are the direct benefits of education. The indirect benefits of education, also known as externalities or spillover benefits, are usually difficult to measure in real terms. Such benefits include reduction in crime, social cohesion, technological innovations and intergenerational benefits.[1]

Education as an investment is divided into two distinct parts. These are the private and social investments. These benefits are shared by the individuals, families, employers, societies and other bodies. The way in which educational investment is shared varies from country to country.

Cost-Benefit Analysis

Cost-benefit analysis is a technique used for evaluating the costs and benefits associated with an investment in order to show its profitability. In education, cost-benefit analysis can be used for making decisions on, for instance, curriculum issues and the system of education to be implemented. An educational investment is considered to be profitable if its expected benefits exceed its costs. Cost-benefit analysis enables educational policy makers to make decisions on which alternative ways of allocating limited resources will produce maximum benefits.[2] However, in making decisions on benefits of education, both the direct and indirect benefits must be considered.

Cost-effectiveness on the other hand, is used when the benefits of an educational programme cannot be estimated in monetary units. Cost-effectiveness is thus a measure of utility of money to achieve a given educational objective.

Budgeting

A budget is an educational programme which is expressed in financial terms. A budget for an educational organisation has an educational plan with an estimate of the amount of money to be received (receipts) and the amount of money to be spent (expenditures) in order to achieve the educational objectives. A budget plan is made for a given period of time, usually one year. A well formulated organisational or school budget should consist of an education plan, an expenditure plan and a revenue plan.

The school budget states (in shillings or dollars) the philosophy and policies of the school system. The budget enables an organisation to determine the quantity and quality of both human and material resources required to enable the organisation to fulfil the purposes for which it was established.

Purposes of the school budget

Estimates of receipts (income) and expenditure (costs)

A budget enables an educational organisation to obtain accurate estimates of the anticipated receipts and expenditures. A well developed budget should enable the educational management to have an accurate forecast of the expected receipts and expenditures during a definite period of time. Estimates of receipts and expenditures also help in balancing the budget which prevents budgetary deficits.

Comprehensive and equitable view of all services

A budget enables an educational organisation to have a comprehensive view of all its services regardless of their magnitude. By analytically looking at all the services equally, the budget thus enables an equitable allocation of financial resources in all the services of an educational organisation.

Basis for accounting

Accounting for funds spent to achieve educational objectives makes it possible to ascertain whether funds have been spent efficiently. The budget plans should therefore help in ensuring efficiency in accounting procedures.

The accounting effectiveness helps in stimulating confidence among parents, educational officials and the school community as a whole.

Determining the quality and quantity of services

Budgeting facilitates a systematic plan for evaluating the quality and quantity of services needed in an educational organisation. The conceptions about what services an educational organisation should provide and the quality and quantity of these services change with the curriculum changes. The educational needs of a society must thus be constantly appraised in keeping with changing needs of the society.

A plan for attaining purposes

A school budget is "a plan for attaining the purposes of an institution"[3]. It is imperative that the purposes for which an organisation was founded must be stated in clear terms. An effective financial management enables an educational organisation to achieve its purpose in the manner desired by the society.

Conferement of authority

A budget plan which has been approved by the responsible bodies provides an educational organisation with the authority to charge fees and other levies, and to spend the monies on the approved items. Educational organisations can only collect monies as stipulated in the approved budget and spend such monies as authorised in the budget plan.

Indeed confidence of parents and the school community in an educational organisation's financial management depends on the meticulous adherence to the budget plan.

Economic administration of an educational organisation

A well planned and executed budget enables educational organisations to be managed in an economical manner. Wastage in financial management overestimates the costs of education and this in turn affects the overall provision of educational services. A budget plan should ensure prudent financial management. This in turn enhances efficiency in the provision of educational services.

Principles of budgeting

In a comprehensive study, Vosecky outlined eleven principles for appraising school budgetary practice.[4] The principles listed below have been derived from this study:

(i) The head-teacher and the board of governors should be responsible for the budget.

(ii) The budget document should be the result of the cooperative efforts of all who are concerned with the educational needs of the students.

(iii) The budget preparation should be a continuous process, with the annual budget being a part of a long-range programme.

(iv) The first step in the preparation of a school budget should be the formulation of a *definite educational plan*.

(v) The second step in the budget formulation and construction should be the preparation of the *spending* or *expenditure plan*, which translates the educational plan into estimated costs.

(vi) The final step in the construction of the budget document is the preparation of the *financing* or *revenue* plan.

(vii) It is the responsibility of the head-teacher to present and interpret the budget to those affected by it.

(viii) The budget should be *adopted* before the beginning of the fiscal year for which it is to serve, but only after the legal body such as a board of governors having power to adopt it has had ample time to analyse and review it.

(ix) After its adoption, the budget should be accurately and carefully recorded in the *official minutes* of the body adopting it.

(x) The administration of the budget is the responsibility of the head-teacher on behalf of the legal body.

(xi) There should be provision for a continuous appraisal of the budget document and the budgetary procedure.

Budget plans

In the school budget, two budget plans are commonly used.

The traditional budget plan

The traditional budget plan has for many years been considered as a document for providing strong fiscal accountability to the public for their funds. In this budget plan, *income* is identified as the first component in school budgeting. However, educational managers are being challenged to justify their financial requests in terms of educational programmes rather than the costs, if education has to compete equitably for public funds.

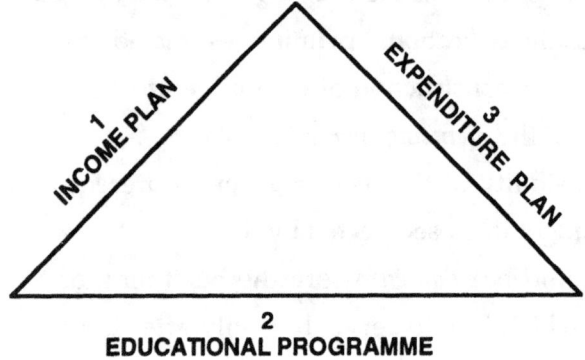

Fig. 16 The traditional budget plan

This budget plan has two major limitations:

(i) the budget plan is structured in order to mainly facilitate income accounting, and the educational programmes are relegated to secondary level. It considers income first, followed by educational programme, and then educational expenditure is considered last (see Figure 16).

(ii) the programme does not emphasise on the cost-benefit analysis of the educational programmes which are either on-going or intended. It is important for educational managers to ascertain the validity of financial allocation to educational programmes. Unnecessary programmes should either be restructured or eliminated and the financial support re-allocated appropriately.

The ideal budget plan

The ideal budget plan identifies the *educational programmes* as the first component, followed by expenditure and then income. This is shown in Figure 17.

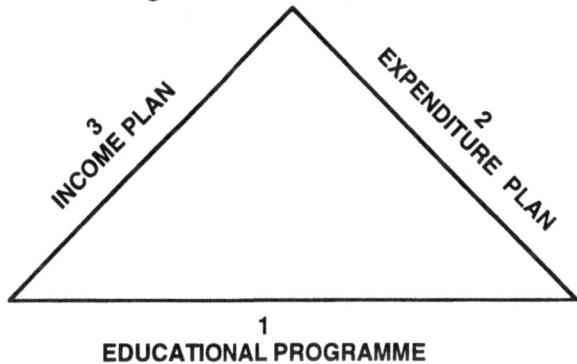

Fig. 17 The ideal budget plan

The ideal budget was established as a result of the shortcomings of the traditional budget. The ideal budget plan has led to the construction of the planning, programming and budgeting systems (PPBS).

The advantages of an ideal budget include:

(i) Directions are given to everybody in the educational organisation as to what the overall objectives and goals are.
(ii) It is participatory in nature.
(iii) Evaluation of educational programmes is made using a wide variety of analytical techniques.
(iv) Emphasis is laid on the output and desired results and so all resources are directed towards the desired results.
(v) Existing and new programmes are continually reviewed and restructured.

The ideal budget plans, however, have two main disadvantages. The first disadvantage is that the long-range projections are subject to miscalculations because of lack of appropriate resources and the unforeseen changes in the future. Secondly, the planning and implementation process may require more staff than the organisation can afford.

The Planning, Programming and Budgeting Systems (PPBS)

Planning, programming and budgeting systems (PPBS) , is a budgeting process in which an educational organisation weighs and analyses the various means by which its objectives can be achieved and an optimum choice among competing alternatives is made. It was first introduced by the U.S. Department of Defence, in 1965. PPBS is an important component of management techniques which are aimed at improving rationality in organisations. It is an interrelated system for providing educational managers with rational information for the analysis of quality and quantity of on-going and intended educational programmes and the financial support necessary for their achievement.

The PPBS enables educational managers to have control over the future needs of education. The budgeting is done for the programmes in the process of systems analysis. The systems analysis is used for critical evaluation of alternative means for achieving organisational objectives. A qualitative analysis of comparable benefits is done in a rational manner so as to implement an optimum choice.

The planning, programming and budgeting systems combines three related but distinct phases:

Planning, which forms the first phase, entails formulation and forecasting of goals and objectives. Planning enables educational managers to highlight the constraints of time, people and material resources necessary for the achievement of objectives.

Programming, which is the second step, is the process of devising the means which are necessary for the achievement of the objectives. A programme might consist of, say, secondary education with its curriculum. Programming helps in the determination and organisation of both human and material resources necessary for organisational effectiveness.

Budgeting refers to the process of transforming the plans and programmes into fiscal terms.

The PPBS uses *systems analysis,* a technique that aids an educational manager in choosing a course of action after systematically investigating costs, objectives, their effectiveness and risks associated with alternative policies. Systems analysis involves both cost-benefit and cost-effective analyses. The analytical process applied enables an educational manager to systematically examine the alternative courses of action in terms of utility and cost, so that relevant alternatives are evaluated.

Characteristics of PPBS

(i) It is *output oriented*. It emphasises the output, by relating programmes to the organisational objectives.

(ii) The *evaluation* is done by comparing desired outcomes with actual accomplishments.

(iii) It applies *quantitative methods* to analyse comparative benefits of programmes. The quantitative methods include cost-benefit analysis, cost-effectiveness evaluation and management information systems.

(iv) It provides the educational manager with a multiplicity of *alternatives* through systems analysis.

(v) It provides a *long-range fiscal planning* in which the annual budgets are integrated in the long-range plans of the organisation.

(vi) It provides for *programme review and revision* which enhance dynamism and innovation in an educational organisation.

(vii) It integrates budgeting in the *policy formulation* in an educational organisation.

(viii) It enhances management *accountability* and *measurement of performance*.

(ix) It provides *economic rationality* in educational organisations. Its analytical techniques enable educational management to provide rationality in economic aspects of educational organisations.

The budgetary process

The school budgetary procedure consists of three main parts:

(a) The educational plan, or programme;
(b) The spending plan, or expenditure or cost; and,
(c) The financial plan, or income or revenue.

The education plan (programme)

The first step in budgeting is the determination of educational plans. The educational plans emanate from the educational policies which are stipulated by the ministry of education. Parliament helps in formulating educational policies. It is imperative that officers responsible for budgeting understand the purposes and policies of education.

The educational plan should include both short and long-term objectives of education. A useful educational plan is one that is specific in order to enable the budget estimates to be reflective.

The budget plan should be able to show:

(i) The age and qualification of students to be admitted and the classes to be completed;
(ii) number of school days;
(iii) student-teacher ratio;
(iv) teacher qualifications;
(v) provision for clinical and guidance departments;
(vi) whether the school is boarding or day; and,
(vii) the required human and material resources in the long run.

The educational plan should thus be comprehensive in order to present a broad view of the educational programme and its purpose. This provides specific information for accurate budgeting.

The expenditure and revenue plans

The budget document should present a comprehensive picture of the anticipated expenditure (costs) and receipts (income).

Expenditure

The school expenditure entails the consideration of the following:

(i) *Contingencies* - financial resources which help in meeting the costs of office equipment, telephone, postage, audit fees, staff uniforms and other necessary office supplies.

(ii) *Instruction* or *school equipment and stores* - expenditure on textbooks, materials *and* equipment required for instruction.

(iii) *Boarding Equipment and stores* - expendable items bought for boarding purposes.

(iv) *Repair, maintenance and improvement* - repairs of original equipment, renovation of school plant and maintenance of equipment and facilities.

(v) *Electricity, water* and *conservancy* - cost of fuel for water or electricity plants, water and electricity bills.

(vi) *Personal emoluments:* salaries and wages to staff employed in the institution. Part-time, overtime and contractual payments are also included here.

(vii) *Local travel and transport* - includes expenditure on transport, subsistence, and fuel costs or mileage claims, insurance and registration of motor vehicles.

(viii) *Other expenditure items* - may be determined by an educational organisation as and when necessary. These may include items like medical, development and library expenditures.

Revenue (income)

Sources of revenue must be well stipulated during budgeting. The revenue sources include:

(i) Grants from the government or other interested agencies.
(ii) Tuition and boarding fees paid by the students.
(iii) House and furniture rents.
(iv) Electricity and water charges recovered from staff.
(v) Activity fees.
(vi) Building fund.
(vii) School farm and other income generating activities.
(viii) Sale of old and obsolete equipment.

The estimates of the receipts and expenditures should be listed in accordance with the revenue sources and expenditure account classification of the accounting system recommended by the ministry of education. This accounting classification is necessary for proper budget administration. The budget should provide room for amendments and improvements. This means that the initial budget document is a *tentative budget* until it is officially approved by the ministry of education or the relevant governing body.

The school management should provide a *budget calendar* at the beginning of each year. The budget calendar includes a schedule showing: responsibilities assigned to different persons and groups; time when each type of information is due; time for assembly of the budget document; time for presenting the tentative budget; and, time for adoption of the budget.

The modern concept of a balanced school budget ensures the balancing of the educational plan along with the expenditures and receipts. A balanced budget is a well proportioned one in which no phase of the school system receives more or less than it needs. Some budget officers may apply *padding* in the budget, which increases the budget by an amount which the adaptors may likely slash off the budget. However, a well balanced budget, whose receipts and expenditure projections can be precisely explained, does not require padding.

In the preparation of the budget, the principal or head-teacher must seek the cooperation of the board of governors, the parents, the teachers and other school employees. By enlisting the cooperation of these people, the principal ensures a comprehensive view of the budget and a feeling of partnership which contributes to the much needed *espirit de corps*.

Presentation, consideration and adoption of the budget

The educational manager should provide ample publicity for the budget document so that the board of governors and the parents association are adequately informed about the budget. The budget should not come out as news to the school community. The board of governors and the parents association must be given ample time to study and consider the budget estimate in detail before it is finally discussed and adopted. The school manager should be able to justify every request in the budget document.

When the board of governors and the parents association are satisfied with the final budget estimate, the principal is authorised to forward the budget to the ministry of education or the relevant body which in turn should approve the budget estimate before the beginning of the year. The approved budget provides the educational manager with authority to collect and spend money necessary for organisational effectiveness. The approved budget also helps to remove any suspicion by the students, teachers and parents which may cause unnecessary unrest in the educational organisation.

Administration of the budget

The administration of the budget involves:
(i) Budget control
(ii) Development of work plans.
(iii) Implementation of the work plans.

Budget control

There must be centralised administration, coordination and control of the budget if the programmes are to be achieved effectively. The central control ensures that those given authority to spend money are kept in check.

The budget estimates must be used constantly in order to guide the financial management in an educational organisation. The budget estimates in each vote-head must be transferred to the top of the appropriate columns in the ledger book. This enables the accounting officer to make quick reference necessary for the control of the various votes.

Work plans

Work plans enable the educational manager to have a clear picture as to who will procure what and when, in accordance with the budget estimates. The work plans must be cognisant of the flow of income available to the organisation. These work plans, which are initiated at the beginning of the year, ensure that the goods and services are procured as and when needed.

Budget administration

In the process of budget administration, the educational manager may realise over-estimates and under-estimates in the various budget items or vote-heads. This may necessitate the acquisition of authority, known as *virement* from the permanent secretary of the ministry of education or the relevant body, to transfer money from one account or vote-head with excess funds to another account or vote-head with less funds.

It is important that the educational manager, together with the board of governors, does not incur deficits unless there is an unforeseen occurrence.

Appraisal of the budget document and the budgetary process

The budget document should be appraised in terms of the purposes for which it was designed. The appraisal should be in terms of:

(i) The extent to which the educational organisation meets its objectives through the budget.
(ii) The provision of accurate and systematic estimate and balance of receipts and expenditure.
(iii) The provision of a comprehensive and an equitable view of all the services in the educational organisation.
(iv) The availability of supplementary information which enables all concerned to understand the budget in totality.
(v) The budget as an important document for financial accounting.

Financial Accounting

Financial accounting is concerned with the maintenance of records in which financial transactions of an educational organisation are summarised. An adequate financial system ensures effective operation in an educational organisation. Financial accounting is thus the process of recording, classifying and summarising financial transactions of an educational organisation and interpreting the results of these transactions.

Financial accounting in an educational organisation serves the following objectives:

(i) It ensures that the financial resources are used for the intended purposes only. It determines the degree of honesty and integrity of the accounting officers.

(ii) It ensures a proper business management for promoting economy.

(iii) It enables educational authorities to have a quick but effective check on both the rate of expenditure and proper financial control.

Book-keeping

Book-keeping is the art of recording business transactions capable of being measured in financial terms.[5] The primary value of book-keeping records is that they are readily available when required.

There are various books of accounts used for book-keeping in educational organisations. These books of accounts are discussed in the next section.

Books of accounts

There are various books of accounts in educational organisations. Some of the books of accounts in use are:
(i) Cash book
(ii) Ledger
(iii) Journal
(iv) Receipt book
(v) Commitment register
(vi) Stores ledgers
(vii) Inventory
(viii) Payment voucher.

The cash book

A cash book is a book of account in which all financial transactions with respect to receipts, payments and banking are recorded. The cash book is written daily so that, through reconciliations, the cash in hand can be checked against the balances reflected in the cash book. The cash book consists of the debit and the credit sections. The debit side is the left hand side of the accounts in which the received money in the form of cash, cheque or postal orders is entered. The credit side is the right hand side of the accounts in which money paid out is entered. In other words the cash book consists of the receipts (debit) and the payments (credit).

The debit and credit columns of the cash book are divided into appropriate columns representing the various vote-heads in operation within an educational organisation. By simply adding transactions in each column we can easily know how much has been received in each vote-head, and we can also find out how much has been spent in each vote-head. The difference between the receipts and payments shows the balance in each vote-head. In the same token, by subtracting the total payments from receipts we can find out the balance of cash in a day, month or year.

The cash book can be used for recording cash and bank transactions in small enterprises like schools. In this case the cash book contains columns for cash and bank on both the debit and credit sides. All moneys received whether in the form of cash, cheque or postal order is entered in the "cash" column on the debit side of the cash book. When money entered in the "cash" column is paid into the bank then the amount must be debited in the "bank" column and credited in the cash column. This is because the bank account receives and the cash gives.

When an educational organisation pays out money by cash, the cash column on the payments (credit) is credited. And when the payments are made by cheque then the bank column is credited on the payments side. In the same token if cash is withdrawn from the bank by means of a cheque then the amount is debited in the cash column of the receipts side and credited in the bank column of the payments side. This is because cash receives and the bank gives. This transaction completes the double-entry book-keeping. In other words, the cash book is a ledger account in which cash transactions are kept outside the ledger. This is because cash transactions are too many to be kept in the ledger, which would in any case be "untidy".

The ledger

The ledger is an extract of all transactions which are recorded in the cash book against each approved vote-head of the estimates. It includes all the adjustments made using the journal. Each page of the ledger, referred to as a ledger account, shows financial transactions for a given vote-head or for a particular person. The various vote-heads are entered in the ledger according to how they appear in the budget estimates.

The simplest form of a ledger account is divided vertically into two sides. The debit is on the left hand side and the credit on the right hand side. The entries appearing in the left hand side, or receipts, of the cash book are credited on the right hand side of the ledger. Similarly, entries appearing on the right hand side, or payments, of the cash book are debited in the left hand side of the ledger. This process is the basis of double-entry book-keeping.

There are two ledger accounts. These are the personal and the impersonal accounts. The personal account records all transactions between the educational organisation and a person or firm with financial dealings in the organisation. The impersonal account records transactions which are non-personal, such as personal emoluments account, boarding equipment account, school equipment account, and contingencies account.

The journal

A journal is a book of accounts which contains records of financial events as they occur in an educational organisation on a daily basis. The sales day, purchase day, sales returns and the purchases returns books are examples of ledgers. However, these are special journals since they record daily transactions. The journal *proper* on the other hand, is used for recording the transactions which cannot be entered into the books of original (prime) entry because of their special nature. These include the purchase of an asset, writing off of bad debts, depreciation of assets and correction of errors in posting from the cash book.

The journal entries are accompanied by a "narration" which provides an explanation of the transaction. The narration is written immediately under the entry.

Receipt books

The receipts are officially printed for the school. They must be in duplicate and serially numbered. A receipt is issued for all monies received by the school. The monies include school fees, grants from the ministry of education or non-governmental organisations and other donors, rents, sales and debtors. The original receipt is given to the person or organisation paying the money, while the duplicate is retained in the receipt book for record and audit purposes.

If an error is made during the writing of a receipt, the cancelled receipt must be retained in its place. Indeed the receipt books are very important documents which show the source of income and must thus be kept under lock and key. All receipts of money, whether in cash, cheque, postal orders or money orders, must be recorded on the left hand side of the cash book; indicating the dates received, source, receipt number, amount and vote-head.

Commitment register (vote book)

The commitment register, or vote book, enables an educational manager to readily verify the amount of money available in each vote-head. All orders placed by an educational organisation must be recorded on the left hand side of the commitment register including their expected expenditure. The right hand side of the commitment register is completed when the goods have been paid for and received. The entries include date, payment voucher number, amount paid and balance, if any. The commitment register is useful in availing information showing that goods ordered have, or have not, been received or paid for. The expected expenditure is taken into account when determining how much money is available in a given vote.

Stores ledger

The numerical balances shown in the stores ledgers at any point in time reflect the actual number of items in the store. There are three categories of stores ledgers: the *permanent stores ledgers*, the *expendable stores ledgers* and the *consumable stores ledger*.

All goods received by an educational organisation must be entered in the appropriate stores ledgers indicating the relevant payment voucher number and amount.

Permanent stores ledgers are stores which have a life exceeding two years. They include furniture, machinery, tools and permanent science equipment.

Expendable stores ledgers are items which are neither permanent nor consumable. They include expendable science equipment such as bottles and glassware; expendable boarding equipment, such as bedding and lightbulbs; expendable stationery such as geometrical instruments and rulers; textbooks in the bookstore or library.

Consumable stores ledgers. These include items which change form or nature when used. They include chemicals, foodstuffs, soap, paint, glue and writing or typing paper.

Inventory

An inventory is a stock register of equipment for both permanent and expendable stores. It enables an educational organisation to have a readily available record of the location and amount of equipment. This assists in curbing unnecessary purchase of duplicate items. Inventory book entries must be made whenever stores are either issued or returned.

The permanent and expendable stores are issued on inventory in which case both the ledger and inventory are entered at the same time, with dates and signatures being made in the correct columns by the relevant officers. All inventory books should be numbered and recorded.

It should be noted that inventory books are not kept for consumable stores, therefore, issues are directly made to the persons requiring them. The persons taking these stores must sign in the relevant column.

The stores' checks, using the inventories, must be done annually in order to ascertain efficiency in the maintenance of stores. The stores' checks must include all items recorded in the inventories.

Payment voucher

All payments made in an organisation must be supported by a payment voucher. A payment voucher contains the payee's name, address and identification number, date, voucher number, invoice number, a brief and clear narration of the reason for payment, amount paid, cheque number, vote-head charged. The payment voucher must be approved by the head of the educational organisation before payment is made. The payment voucher number and other details are used for completing the payments section of the cash book.

Supporting receipts, signed agreements or invoices must be firmly attached to the original payment voucher which is filed in a sequential order. The duplicate copy of the payment voucher is given to the payee.

It should be noted that at the bottom of invoices and receipts is an expression E.&O.E. "errors and omissions excepted". This reminds the buyer that the details stated in the invoice or receipt are not final, since any errors detected later may have to be "corrected"

Double entry book-keeping

In the double entry book-keeping there is recognition of the twofold aspect of every financial transaction in an educational organisation. Double entry book-keeping is completed when the cash book records are transferred to relevant columns in the ledger. The entries which appear in the left hand (or receipts or debit) side of the cash book are posted in the right hand or credit column of the ledger. On the other hand, entries which appear in the right hand (or payments or credit) side of the cash book are posted in the left hand or debit column of the ledger. This is to say that every debit entry in the cash book has a corresponding credit entry in the ledger, and likewise, every credit entry in the cash book has a corresponding debit entry in the ledger.

The basic rule of double entry book-keeping is that the *account which receives is debited* whereas *the account which gives is credited*. In other words, what comes into the account is debited and what goes out of the account is credited. When a transaction is posted from the cash book to a ledger, then the relevant folio number appearing in the cash book is entered in the folio column of the ledger. This facilitates quick reference. Double entry book-keeping helps in ascertaining the accuracy of the book-keeping system.

Advantages of double entry book-keeping

(i) It provides an arithmetical check of the accuracy of the book-keeping, since both sides of the ledger must be equal in their total.

(ii) It provides a complete record of financial transactions in an educational organisation.

(iii) It helps in detection and prevention of errors and frauds in an educational organisation.

(iv) It helps in the preparation of a trial balance and hence a balance sheet.

(v) It enables an educational organisation to find out its losses or profits in income-generating activities. Excess of credit balance over debit balance shows a, profit, and the reverse shows a loss.

The trial balance

The trial balance enables an educational organisation to ascertain the accuracy and objectivity of the financial accounting data so far obtained. It is compiled once a month. At the end of the financial period a balance sheet is extracted from the books of account in order to show the financial state of the educational organisation. However, before the balance sheet can be prepared, it is necessary to test, as far as possible, the accuracy of the financial records from which it is made. The trial balance enables the organisation to determine the true position of its financial records.

The trial balance shows a list of all the balances which appear at any given date of the month in the ledger and the cash book of an educational organisation. The principle behind a trial balance is that when the debit and credit entries are made in the ledger without any errors, then the total of debits must equal the total of credits at any given time. The agreement of these totals confirms the arithmetical accuracy of the financial records thus far. The trial balance also helps in providing information useful for the preparation of the profit and loss account.

It should be noted that the agreement of the trial balance's data does not mean that the information is error-free. Errors may still occur as a result of either complete omission of transactions from books, posting to wrong accounts, compensation errors, or errors of principle. A trial balance should be made by educational organisations at the end of each month and copies sent to the relevant departments of the ministry of education.

The trial balance columns include vote-head, ledger folio number, debit, credit, commitments and balance of money available as at the end of the month.

Balance sheet

The balance sheet is a summary of the ledger account balances remaining in the books of accounts. The assets, which are the debit balances in the books are shown on the right hand side, and the liabilities and capital account, which are credit balances in the books, on the left hand side. This is the reverse of the ledger documentation.

The balance sheet is thus a statement which shows, on the one hand, the amount and source of capital employed in the educational organisation, and on the other hand, the form in which such capital is employed. The fixed assets are valued at cost, less depreciation, while the current assets are also valued at cost.

The balance sheet, which is made at the end of the accounting period or year, does not in real terms show the current monetary worth of the educational organisation. This is because the values indicated for the assets may not be their actual selling worth at the date of the balance sheet. In addition, the value of goodwill by parents and other interested parties is usually overlooked.

Cash and bank reconciliation

At the end of every month, totals in the cash and bank columns are worked out in the cash book for both the debit and credit sides. Indeed, the debit totals should equal the credit totals. The cash and bank balances are carried to the next page, for the beginning of a new month. This is done after the bank reconciliation statement has been made.

The *bank reconciliation statement* enables the educational organisation to confirm the details in the cash book with respect to bank statements at the end of each month. The bank thus supplies the educational organisation with the details of the *statement of accounts* for the month in question. The bank statement of accounts is a copy of the ledger account of the educational organisation in the books of the bank. The amounts paid into the bank are shown on the credit side, and the mounts withdrawn are shown on the debit side. In other words, the bank statement records are the reverse of the cash book records.

In most cases it will be found that the bank balance as shown in the statement of account, at a given time, differs with the cash book records.

This may be as a result of:

(i) Certain cheques received by the educational organisation may not have been banked, even though they are debited in the cash book.

(ii) Some cheques which have already been banked may not have been recorded in the bank statement.

(iii) Some payees may not have presented their cheques to the bank.
(iv) Certain cheques may have been "dishonoured" for one reason or the other.
(v) Bank charges may have been entered into the statement but not in the cash book.

In the bank reconciliation statement it is necessary that a comparison is made between the cash book debits with the bank statement's credits, and the credit in the cash book with the debits in the bank statement, by ticking. Any receipts or payments in the bank statement not yet in the cash book should be entered in the cash book at the beginning of the following month in the bank column.

Table 1 below shows an example of a bank reconciliation statement "for the year 19x1".

Table 1. Bank reconciliation statement, as at 31st July 19x1

	KSh	KSh
Balance as per bank statement		140,000.20
Less unpresented cheque No. CA 1000	2,000.00	
Less unpresented cheque No. CA 1001	1,500.00	
Less unpresented cheque No. CA 1002	2,000.00	5,500.00
		134,500.20
Add deposits not credited	3,000.00	3,000.00
Balance as per cash book		137,500.20

Verified and certified correct
Signed

Manager/Finance Officer, etc.

Dishonoured cheques

When a deposited or banked cheque is returned unpaid, then the following process should be effected. The amount of the cheque is credited in the bank column and the same amount is debited in the cash column of the cash book. The drawer must be asked to pay in cash immediately. Indeed it is strongly advised that cheques must be deposited to the bank immediately, so that they do not become stale.

Suspense account

A suspense account has three main functions:
(i) It provides an account to which a transaction can be posted until its correct destination is known. For instance, when a bank note in settlement of an account is received without a covering letter. In this case the amount is posted from the debit side of the cash book to the credit side of the suspense account until the name of the sender is known. When the name of the sender is known then the suspense account is debited and the sender's account is credited.
(ii) It provides an account for deferred expenses.
(iii) It provides an account to which any difference on the trial balance can be posted pending discovery of errors. When the errors are detected they are corrected by debiting and crediting the suspense account.

Clearance account

It is necessary that some statutory deductions which are made on monthly basis are transacted using a clearance account, instead of the suspense account. These deductions include PAYE, NHIF, NSSF and service charge.

These deductions are debited in the cash column of the cash book, and credited in the individual clearance accounts. When these deductions are paid to the respective authorities, the cash book is credited and the clearance accounts are debited.

Income generating account

Educational organisations are expected to be involved in income generating activities which enable them to have supplementary sources of income necessary for their daily financial commitments. This is because of the central government's reduction of its financial assistance to educational institutions. An income generating account should thus be opened.

Some of the income generating activities which educational organisations are, or can be, involved in include:

(i) Milk production from dairy cows.
(ii) Beef production from beef cattle.
(iii) Pork production from pigs.
(iv) Egg and chicken production from poultry.
(v) Crop production - coffee, tea, maize, beans or kale.
(vi) Furniture production by the craft department.
(vii) Training and consultancy activities.

The income generating account should show the *profit and loss account*. The *net profit* in the accounting period is obtained by deducting all expenses incurred in producing, selling and distributing goods, and in managing and financing the income generating activities from tne gross profit. It should be noted that an income generating activity that shows no net profit, after all mismanagement loopholes have been sealed, is not worth the sacrifice, and should thus be discontinued.

Auditing

Auditing deals with the investigation of the financial records of an educational organisation in order to ascertain the objectivity and accuracy of the financial statements. Auditing is thus an activity which appraises the accuracy and completeness of the accounting system applied by an educational organisation.

Objectives of auditing

It should be noted that the main purpose of auditing is not to uncover mismanagement or embezzlement of the funds. The major objectives of auditing are:

(i) To determine whether the financial statements made by an educational organisation are accurate in both calculations of figures and in application of the recommended accounting guidelines.

(ii) To determine whether an educational organisation uses procedures which comply with the legal provisions, policies and procedures stipulated by the ministry of education or the relevant body.

(iii) To identify any operational problems in the accounting procedure used by the educational organisation so as to provide remedial recommendation for improvement.

Internal and external auditing

Internal auditing

Educational managers must institute proper administrative structures for internal auditing. It is recommended that there should be an officer whose duty is to perform the tasks of internal auditing. This is because internal auditing enables an organisation to appraise the effectiveness of its financial management techniques and control. Internal auditing is thus an important financial management control device.

The educational manager is expected to be conversant with auditing techniques within the organisation. This is because he or she may help in detecting financial management flaws before it is too late to alleviate them.

External auditing

External auditing is performed by agencies from outside the educational organisation. The main aim of external auditing is to ascertain that the organisation has complied with the stipulated financial control mechanisms. It is only fitting that an independent body ensures that all the financial controls which include internal auditing have adhered to the stipulated guidelines.

Internal auditing helps in either making recommendations regarding deficiencies and suggestions for improvement or identifying shortfalls and giving suggestions for investigations.

Contrasting accounting and auditing

From the foregoing discussions it is apparent that accounting and auditing are closely related. This is because auditing provides a financial opinion on the financial statements of an organisation. These financial statements are the products of the accounting system obtained in the organisation.

The auditors' work involves scrutiny of the accounting data in order to ascertain their accuracy and objectivity. In doing this the auditor analyses and reviews the details in the accounting documents; indeed the auditor's job requires a comprehensive analysis of the financial management of the entire organisation.

The data found in the accounting documents provide the auditor with the information necessary for making judgements on the effectiveness of the financial management techniques. The accounting data thus provide an auditor with raw data necessary for this task. The auditor is concerned with the validity of the data in the accounting documents as well as the clerical accuracy of the documentation.

Auditing procedures

Foremost in the task of the auditor is that he or she must have a thorough knowledge of the educational organisation whose financial documents are to be audited. This knowledge includes the organisation's sources of financing, its structure and its unique aspects. The knowledge of the structure of the organisation helps in detecting weaknesses which may provide unreliable and fraudulent records. This prior knowledge enables the auditor to understand the accounting documents prepared by the organisation.

Audit procedures include:

Observation

To get first hand information about an educational organisation the auditor simply observes the existence of the entities in question. He or she can simply observe whether a building, land or an equipment is available. The actual operational behaviours of individuals involved in financial management is also observed in relation to their impact on the production of financial documents. In case of cash in hand, the auditor observes it by actually counting the money.

Inquiry

In the process of auditing the auditor asks pertinent questions in order to get further information or clarification. Inquiry may involve face to face interviewing or written reports.

Confirmation

This is a type of inquiry in which an auditor obtains written statements from companies outside the organisation or individuals who are both reliable and knowledgeable on the issues of interest. For instance, the auditor may have to confirm the undelivered goods from the suppliers or actual funds in the bank from the bank manager.

Retracing data processing

If the auditor wants to discover an error made in an accounting process, then he or she can repeat the accounting process step by step. This may involve tracing transactions from the cash book to the ledger to ascertain accurate postings.

Recomputation

As opposed to retracing, recomputation helps to determine the arithmetical calculations in the data processing by recalculating the results.

Vouching

The vouching procedure involves the actual examination of documents such as invoices and delivery notes and then comparing the documents with the accounting records. The idea is that the accounting records are the results of purchases and receipts.

Ratio and trend analysis

This is the process of compiling financial statements ratios for the year in question and comparing these with those of previous years. If the ratios for some items of the year in question differ significantly with those of the previous years then there is reason for in-depth investigations.

Summary

This chapter begins with an overview of financial management in education. Education is viewed as both a private and a social investment whose financing must thus be met by both the individual and the society. Educational managers should be conversant with, and apply, cost-benefit analysis as an important tool for determining alternative ways of allocating limited resources to produce maximum benefits.

The budget, its purposes, principles, plans, processes are been discussed in this chapter. The planning, programming and budgeting systems, as an example of an ideal budget plan, is also discussed. The basic concept is that the educational plans are considered first before developing the expenditure and the income plans.

On financial accounting, various books of accounts commonly used in educational organisations are discussed. The double entry book-keeping, the trial balance, and the balance sheet are also discussed here. This section ends with an elucidation on bank reconciliation, suspense, clearance and income generating accounts.

The last part of the chapter deals with auditing; its objectives, types and procedures.

END NOTES

[1] B. Weisbrod, *External Benefits of Public Education: An Economic Analysis.* Princeton, New Jersey: Princeton University, Industrial Relations Section, 1964.

[2] G. Psacharopoulos and M. Woodhall, *Education and Development: An analysis of Investment Choices,* A World Bank Publication, New York: Oxford University Press, 1985, p. 333.

[3] A.J. Burke, *Financing of Public Schools in the U.S.* New York: Harper and Row Publishers, 1957, p. 34.

[4] E.W. Vosecky, "A study of bbudgetary procedures in selected East Tennessee county school systems", Doctoral Dissertation, University of Tennessee, 1957.

[5] R.E.G. Perrins, *Practical Book-Keeping,* 1st Edition. London: HFL Publishers Ltd, 1972, p. 1.

HUMAN RESOURCE DEVELOPMENT IN EDUCATIONAL MANAGEMENT

Human resource development in educational management is the process by which educational managers identify, develop and effectively release the maximum potentials of employees for the benefit of both the organisation, and the individual workers.

The Human Resources in Educational Organisations

In an educational organisation, human resources include the workers and the students. The workers here consist of the teaching and the non-teaching staff. The combined effort of workers and students is aimed at enhancing teaching and learning in the educational organisation.

The *teachers* are probably the most important resource that any country has. This is because an efficient human capital development depends on the quality and effectiveness of teachers. The quality of the doctors, teachers, lawyers, accountants, engineers and other professionals depends on how well they have been prepared for their various roles in the society by their teachers. Teachers thus play a key role in the overall human resource development in any country.

There is, however, a strong indication that most teachers in both primary and secondary schools in developing countries have been conscripted into the teaching profession due to their inability to gain entry into other professions. This implies that the teaching profession in developing countries has two lots of teachers: those who chose the profession for intrinsic reasons, and those who, for reasons beyond their control, have found themselves in the profession. Therefore, a main issue in human resource development for teachers is that a good proportion of them enter the teaching profession with low morale. A consciously designed human resource development effort is, therefore, a must if the work motivation and job satisfaction are to be improved to make all teachers "willing professionals".

The *non-teaching* or supporting staff in an educational organisation are those employees who provide the support services. They include registrars, bursars, accountants, clerks, matrons, secretaries, typists, foremen, janitors, cooks, watchmen and cleaners. Indeed, these workers' duties ensure that teaching and learning environment is made conducive for the attainment of the educational objectives. A well designed procedure for effective and efficient integration of these employees within the teaching and learning environment is imperative if the objectives for which the educational organisations were established are to be achieved.

In order for the supporting staff to be effectively involved in the achievement of the educational objectives, their potentials need to be consciously detected, developed and released. The supporting staff members play a very crucial role in any educational organisation and so their roles must be seen within the context of an integral system.

The *students* in educational organisations are the raw materials in the education industry. Students also form a very significant part of the human resource. They are the ones who learn; in addition, the students are the ones through whom the educational objectives are achieved.

The students in educational organisations should thus form an integral part of the human resource development programme. A number of students are, or should be, appointed to positions of leadership such as prefect and captain, which provide educational management and the students with an important link. The students' representatives, within the educational management, can perform their roles effectively if their potentials are consciously developed in planned forums, such as seminars, debates and speech days. The human resource development strategies discussed in the next sub-topics, however, deal with the employees of educational organisations only.

Educational managers are faced with an onerous task of ensuring that the workers who are in their organisations, either by choice or default, are provided with an environment which is professionally motivating and satisfying. The work environment should be able to provide hope and assurance through an appropriate career structure, so that even the "unwilling professionals" are positively assimilated into the profession.

Staffing an educational organisation adequately is not just a matter of having all the staff positions filled. The workers must be enabled to fit into the various job demands which constantly change due to curricular improvements and research effort. Since human resources are perishable resources, they have to be developed and utilised at the right time. Workers who are a great resource at the moment will depreciate in the near future. Therefore, their resourcefulness must be fully developed and utilised at the moment, not only to achieve the immediate needs of the education system, but also to help in preparing other workers who will fill the positions in future.

Educational organisations must prepare for their future staff needs through strategic human resource planning. Educational organisations must also assure their teachers and other employees that there will be opportunities for them to develop their careers in a manner that will be in congruence with their goals and aspirations. Educational managers must thus ensure that the desire for educational organisations to develop the workers and the workers' desire to develop themselves in their work assignments do not oppose but reinforce each other. For workers to be effectively integrated into their educational organisations, there must be a convergence between their career goals and the organisations' staff development plans. When there is lack of employee-organisation integration due to inappropriate human resource development strategies, then there will be ineffectiveness and dissatisfaction among workers.

Career Development

A career refers to a sequence of positions, jobs or occupations that one person engages in during his or her working life. It is an individually perceived sequence of attitudes and behaviours associated with work-related experiences and activities over the span of a person's life.[1]

Thus, a career does not imply success or failure. It is a series of life-long events as experienced by a worker in his or her work place, but not an evaluation of how successful or unsuccessful he or she has been. The work-related experiences for an employee may include a series of promotions in the organisation or in the entire education system.

Schein has identified five primary career anchors, which are factors that cause people to seek certain types of work.[2] The five anchors are:

(1) Technical or functional competence — whereby workers are excited by the work itself;
(2) Managerial competence — where workers enjoy the exercise of power;
(3) Security and stability — where workers are motivated by security and long-term careers in one firm;
(4) Creativity or entrepreneurship — where workers enjoy launching their own business enterprises, and
(5) Autonomy and independence — where workers desire freedom from organisational constraints.

The idea of career anchors can help educational managers to better understand the career paths chosen by employees in order to direct their training needs accordingly.

There are four main stages in the career development of an employee.

(a) The exploration stage

This is the period that begins prior to employee's entry into a profession, during school days or when he or she is looking for a job. It is the time when a potential employee is assessing the various job alternatives. The exploration stage continues for a few months or years into the work environment, during which time employees begin questioning whether they made the correct job choice or not. The exploration stage goes upto the age of 25 years.

(b) The establishment stage

This is the stage when employees gain an in-depth understanding of their assigned job and the professional demands of the work assignment. Employees then strive to make their impact in their organisations. The establishment stage is also the stage when employees get assimilated into the human environment. For the educational organisation, this is the time to evaluate the professional worth of the workers. The establishment stage goes upto the age of 35 years.

(c) The maintenance stage

This is the stage when employees have entrenched themselves in their profession. It is difficult for a majority of workers to leave their profession at this stage due to their long investment in their job career and low marketability as a result of age. This is a very crucial stage for both the workers and the educational managers because it is either now or never for both the employee and the profession. This stage goes upto 45 years.

(d) The decline stage

This is the depreciation stage when the employees' professional and physical abilities begin to wane as they approach their retirement. Educational managers need to be acutely aware of the human resource development strategies for the employees at this time when their maximum potentials have already elapsed. And yet this is the time when an explicit human resource management can *milk the workers dry* of their remaining but crucial potentials. This stage goes up to 60 years (see Figure 18).

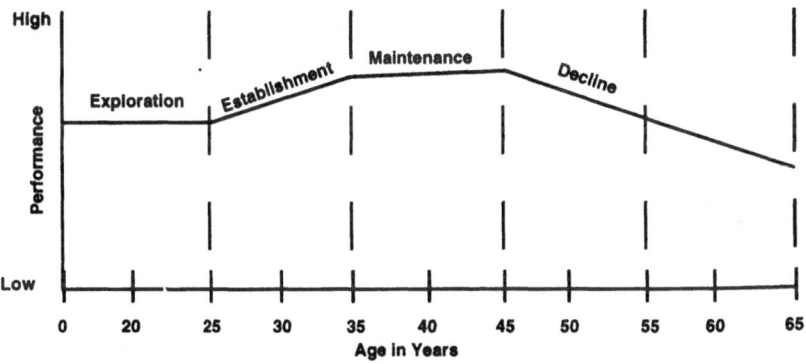

Fig. 18 Stages in career development

Job Analysis, Job Description and Job Specification

Job analysis

Job analysis involves developing a detailed description of the tasks involved in a job, determining the relationship between the job and other jobs in the educational organisation and setting out the academic abilities and professional skills of the employees which are necessary for performing the job. The foremost task in educational management is to undertake a thorough job analysis since this forms a fundamental foundation upon which human resource development strategies are based.

Job description

Job description refers to a written statement of what a job holder does, how it is done, and why it is done.[3] A job description, thus, defines the scope of responsibility and continuing work assignment which are sufficiently different from those of other jobs to warrant a specific title.[4] An employee's job should be very clearly spelt out so that conflicts that may arise from role ambiguity are avoided. An objective performance appraisal is based on a well thought-out job description.

Job specification

After a written job description, it is important that educational managers specify the minimum acceptable qualifications that a worker must possess so as to perform the defined job successfully. This is what is referred to as a job specification. A job specification must define in details the academic and professional qualifications which are required of the worker in order for him or her to perform the job effectively. The job specification also includes certain personality requirements and interpersonal skills which are required of a job holder. Such interpersonal skills like negotiation, conversation, compromise and tactfulness should form a significant part of a job specification, since jobs in educational institutions require workers to deal with a diverse clientele ranging from students, teachers, parents, politicians to the members of the general public.

It is an important task of job specification to paint a picture of the type of a worker required to fill a specific job. Job specification is also known as person specification.

Functions of job analysis and job description

Job analysis and job description perform the following functions:

(i) During the workers' recruitment, selection and placement, the educational managers can use the information from job analysis and job description to get the right teachers for each job.

(ii) Job description helps during the orientation or induction of new employees. It helps to clarify what a new worker needs to know about his or her new task assignment. As has already been said before, this helps to prevent misunderstandings which can be avoided. A job description is a reliable impersonal guide for both the employee and his or her immediate supervisor.

(iii) Job description is an important check-list which is very useful during performance appraisal. The duties, expectations, difficulties and misunderstandings are best discussed between employees and their immediate supervisors on the basis of objective job descriptions. Job descriptions also help individual workers to have their own self-appraisal and self development.

(iv) Job description is a very important tool for both promotion and transfer of employees. A well designed job description helps educational managers to decide when a worker is due for promotion on the basis of his or her job performance or when his or her experience can best be utilised elsewhere.

(v) Job description helps educational managers to take disciplinary measures against workers who have not performed their jobs as required of them.

(vi) Job description is a useful tool for employees' salary administration. Comprehensive and objective job descriptions form a factual basis for educational managers during the grading of all the jobs and the determination of a salary structure which is both internally and externally equitable.

Recruitment, Selection and Placement

Recruitment

Recruitment refers to the process of making a worker interested in a particular job so as to apply for it. It is a positive process of searching for prospective workers and stimulating them to apply for these jobs. The recruitment process is undertaken after the manpower requirement process has shown need for new workers or promotions of the incumbents.

In developing countries, there is a general tendency to employ teachers directly from the teacher training colleges or universities without following the time-tested personnel management procedures. This has been so because of the high population growth rate which has placed a lot of pressure on the educational facilities. Since there has been a great demand for teachers at all levels of schooling in developing countries, it has been difficult to use the recruitment process to either choose who should become a teacher or improve the competitiveness of the teaching jobs. The recruitment of non-teaching staff does not have the problems inherent in the recruitment of teachers.

Whereas educational managers in developing countries may be grappling with the problem of applying their well designed human resource management techniques during teacher-recruitment, it is, nevertheless, important that the recruitment process is undertaken in educational management. To make the teaching profession competitive there must be a concerted effort to make those who have been trained to become teachers compete for the teaching positions.

The recruitment of teachers should begin from the school time, when students make their decisions to become teachers on the basis of the values which they attach to the teaching profession. It is, thus, an important task of educational management to make the teaching profession attractive enough for prospective teachers to develop their interests at a very early age. This first step in recruitment of teachers entails making prospective teachers attracted to the teaching profession via teacher training. The first step in the recruitment of teachers is thus the *professional recruitment*. This is the beginning of human resource development in the teaching profession.

When an educational manager has determined that there is need to fill up a particular position and he or she has been given the approval by the management board to have the position filled, then the next step is to determine the recruitment sources. There are two recruitment sources, namely *internal* and *external*. The internal recruitment source is important for promotions, and it has many motivational and job satisfaction advantages among employees. The other advantage of internal recruitment source is that it reduces the costs which may be incurred from recruitment to training. A major disadvantage of internal recruitment is that of inbreeding.

The external source is resorted to when a particular position requires a worker whose qualification is not possessed by the available work force, or when some vacant staff positions require filling with new employees. There are many methods used in external recruitment. The first method is direct advertising in the newspapers. Although advertisements are expensive, they have the potential of reaching a wider market and this increases the chances of getting the most appropriate applicant for the position advertised. The second method of worker recruitment is by making direct contact with a particular training college or university. Educational managers should make special efforts to establish and maintain professional links with college administrators or university faculties.

Other methods of external recruitment include: private employment bureaux, introductions by existing staff, government employment agencies and head-hunting.[5] In head-hunting, an educational manager may poach an employee of rare talent or expertise from another organisation by offering him or her better employment terms.

When the recruitment process has been undertaken, educational managers should evaluate the successes and failures of the recruitment strategy undertaken. The recruitment strategy should be evaluated in terms of the number of those applying, attraction of the right employees, the number of workers actually employed, the cost-benefit analysis, and the successful placement of the employees.

Selection

Selection is the process of matching individual employees to the jobs they have applied for. In the matching process the applicants' qualifications are rated against the specifications of the job advertised. The selection process is very crucial in human resource development, because if the task of employee-job fit is not achieved then both the organisation and the individual worker will suffer for obvious reasons.

In the selection process many methods are available for finding out important information about workers to be employed. These methods include interviews and various written tests, such as intelligence tests, aptitude tests, achievement tests and personality tests.

Interview

The interview is by far the most commonly used selection method. And yet it is the most abused selection device. The main reason why the interview is widely abused is the belief that anybody can conduct an interview. For the interviewers to be effective, they need to be thoroughly trained in the fundamental rules of good interviewing. The results of an interview usually carry a disproportionate impact in the selection decision. This is to say that the interviewee who performs poorly in an interview has very few chances of getting the job, regardless of his or her professional and academic qualifications.

The interview can, therefore, be a poor selection device if it is poorly applied. Research indicates that prior knowledge about an applicant biases the interviewers' evaluation, that interviewers tend to favour applicants who share their attitudes, that the order in which the applicants are interviewed influences the evaluations, that negative information is given unduly high weight and that the applicant's ability to do well in an interview is irrelevant in most jobs.[6] Since interviews are very useful tools for assessing applicants intelligence, interpersonal skills and level of motivation, they are good for the selection of applicants for jobs which require these skills.

Interviewing should be seen as a two-way process for both the organisation and the interviewee. In the first instance, it should enable the organisation to assess whether the interviewee is willing and able to do the job successfully. On the other hand, the interviewee should also be afforded the opportunity to assess whether the job and the organisation are suitable for him or her. The following are some of the important guidelines to be taken into consideration by the interviewers:

(i) Interviews should be held in comfortable surroundings free from interruption.
(ii) The interviewer must be conversant with all the data concerning both the job and the applicant beforehand.

(iii) The interview must be clearly based on both job description and job specification.
(iv) There must be an agreed upon criterion in a check-list form for rating the applicants.
(v) The interview should provide an enabling environment for the applicant so that he or she is relaxed throughout the interview. The mental setting should be that of rapport.
(vi) The questions asked during the interview should be as open-ended as possible.
(vii) The interviewer should be very attentive throughout the interview, and should avoid reacting in a manner that openly reveals disapproval.
(viii) The leads from the interviewee should be consciously followed in order to probe pertinent areas in depth.
(ix) The interviewer must not be influenced by "halo effects."

Written tests

The main purpose of employment tests is to enable management to predict what a person will do in the future by measuring selected psychological factors. The use of written tests has not been popular in many organisations since it is difficult to validate that these tests are job-related. A fundamental task of educational management, however, is to ensure that tests which are used are consistently job-related. This section discusses the intelligence tests, aptitude tests, achievement tests, personality tests and performance simulation tests.

Intelligence tests are probably the most widely used standardised tests by management. Intelligence tests measure reasoning, word fluency, comprehension, numeracy, memory and object assembly. The intelligence tests are usually designed to cover several areas of intelligence and are marked and ranked against contemporaries.

Aptitude tests measure whether an applicant has the capacity or potential to learn a given job if he or she is provided with an enabling environment. Aptitude tests are generally more relevant when applied to prospective applicants before they are trained.

Achievement tests measure how effective an applicant has been in his or her profession in the past. Whereas aptitude tests measure the capacity of a worker to learn in the future, the achievement tests are concerned with what a worker has already accomplished. An achievement test is a good predictor of the performance of a worker in the future, because the performance in the past should be an indicator of what the future performance is likely to be.

Personality tests are used for measuring workers' interests, ideas and beliefs. Personality tests are very important in the teaching profession because an employee's job involves interacting with very diverse clientele. However, it is important to point out that these tests are very difficult to administer and should only be used after careful planning.

Performance simulation tests are also important selection tests which need to be mentioned here. These tests provide the applicants with an opportunity to do the job in a simulated environment. The idea in performance simulation tests is that the best way to find out if an applicant can do a job successfully is to let him or her actually do it.

Placement

Placement refers to the process of matching the employee to both the content and the context of the assigned job, when an employment offer has been made. It is, however, difficult to match a new employee, about whom very little is still known, to the various aspects of the job. Therefore, during the early stages of employment an employee is still on probation, pending an appraisal report from the immediate supervisor. Placement is also known as orientation, induction or initiation

During the placement period there is need for the management to enable the new employee to go through a well designed induction or orientation programme. A consciously designed programme should be made to assist the new employee to settle on the job as smoothly as possible. The induction process must give the details of the job description and the overall organisational expectations of work-related activities. The new employee should be introduced to all staff and students. The worker should also be exposed to the various work-related and social facilities. A successful placement programme ensures that the recruitment and selection processes are not wasteful efforts.

Training, Development and Performance Appraisal

Training and development

Training is the process of providing junior employees with specific knowledge and skills in order to enable them to perform specific work tasks. Development, on the other hand, is the process of providing senior employees with conceptual skills for performing general duties. Whereas training provides employees with specific skills for specific duties, development provides conceptual skills for general duties. For instance, employees may be trained on the newer techniques of stimulus variations in the classroom, or on the methods of managing discussion groups in the lower classes. On the other hand, employees may be given development courses on the concepts of human resource development, or on the philosophy of humanising the work environment. Training, therefore, implies the provision of specific skills to the middle and the lower cadre of workers, and development implies the provision of general and conceptual skills to the upper cadres of workers. In this section, the terms training and development are used interchangeably. The reader is, however, required to conceptualise the distinctions made.

Educational management has no choice as to whether to train employees or not. All employees, regardless of their previous training, education and experience must be given further training and development. This is because the competence of workers will never last forever, due to such factors as curriculum and technological changes, transfers and promotions. Training and development are, therefore, a must in educational management and so the only choice for educational managers is the methodology: whether to have consciously designed training and development programmes or to have them in an haphazard and casual manner. It is important for educational managers to note that if no definite programme of training is planned then there will be higher training costs not only because employees will take too long to learn the required skills, but also because of the likelihood that they will not learn the best methods necessary for their specific assignments.

Training of workers serves the following important functions:

(i) Training is an important investment in human resources since it increases employees' productivity. Acquisition of newer skills and knowledge helps employees to increase both quantity and quality of output in their work.

(ii) Training enhances job motivation and satisfaction. Dissatisfaction which leads to tardiness, absenteeism, turnover and job restriction can be greatly reduced when employees are enabled, through training, to experience direct job satisfaction associated with a sense of achievement and the knowledge that they are developing their inherent capabilities at work.

(iii) Training reduces the problems which are associated with the supervision of employees. This is because a well designed training programme enhances employees' abilities to learn new work methods and equipment and also helps them to adjust to changes in the content and context of their jobs.

(iv) Training increases a worker's value to an organisation, and this prepares him or her for promotion.

(v) Training increases the stability of an educational organisation since it creates a reservoir of qualified employees who easily replace those who either transfer, retire or exit from the organisation for various reasons.

(vi) Training reduces work-related accidents. This is because proper training in job skills and safety techniques enhances employee abilities to handle work-related equipment carefully.

There are two types of training methods. These are on-the-job and off-the-job training methods.

On-the-job training. In this type of training a new employee learns various aspects of his or her job while at the same time actually performing these tasks. For on-the-job training to be successful, the trainers must be well qualified on instructional methodologies. Employees are able to translate their theoretical work skills better into practice during their actual performance if educational managers provide them with the conditions which promote on-the-job training. Some of the on-the-job training methods include: apprenticeship, job rotation, mentoring or coaching and understudy.

In *apprenticeship* a worker learns a wide variety of skills under the guidance of an experienced employee. For this method to be successful the senior employee or instructor must be very skilled in the work methods.

Job rotation involves the lateral transfer of employees to work on different job assignments. This helps in broadening the background of workers and helps them to see the inter-relatedness among the various aspects of an educational organisation.

Mentoring, or *coaching,* is a kind of apprenticeship for senior positions. In this case a senior member of staff assumes responsibility for the career development of his or her subordinate. It is a close and long-term work relationship.

In *understudy*, one employee is specifically designated the role of the heir apparent. Here a trainee learns from his or her superior with the aim of taking over the responsibility in the future.

Off-the-job training. These are training methods which workers undergo outside their work environments. These include: special courses or classes, role-playing, sensitivity training, simulation, vestibule training, conference training and special meetings.

Special courses can be designed by an educational organisation itself or they can be developed by a college or university. In *role-playing,* employees are trained to perform specific work roles, like that of an instructional supervisor. The *sensitivity training* is aimed at increasing the general awareness and sensitivity to behavioural patterns of ones self and others. *Simulations* involve the imitations, or simulation of a real-life situation. Role-playing and case studies are examples of simulations. A *vestibule training* is a method whereby employees learn their jobs on the same equipment which they will be using in their specific jobs. Attempts are made in vestibule training to duplicate the work conditions as much as possible.

Performance appraisal

Performance appraisal refers to the evaluation of the effectiveness of workers in their work assignments. It is aimed at finding out the potentials of an individual employee. Performance appraisal helps in evaluating how a worker succeeds in his present job and this is important for estimating how well he or she will perform in the future. It is different from job evaluation which appraises the job itself and its comparative monetary worth.

Performance appraisal has the following functions:

(i) It helps in determining the strengths and weaknesses of individual workers so that remedial measures can be taken to improve productivity.
(ii) It enables management to determine training needs of workers as individuals or as groups.
(iii) It provides a basis for promotion, transfers or dismissals.
(iv) It helps in increasing job satisfaction of workers by developing their potentials through proper feedback mechanisms.
(v) It is an important tool for human resource planning in an educational organisation.
(vi) It is an important source of feedback on the effectiveness of selection and training.
(vii) Performance appraisal helps educational researchers to carry out research in the most crucial areas inorder to provide solutions to educational problems.

The following are the main performance appraisal methods:

Written essays

In written essays an immediate supervisor of a worker is asked to describe the workers strengths, weaknesses and potentials. This method of appraisal depends heavily on the objectivity of the supervisor.

Critical incidents

In the critical incidents method a supervisor describes, in writing, a good or bad thing that a worker did at a particular time. In this case only specific behaviours are cited. From this kind of listing a worker can be shown his or her strengths and weaknesses.

Graphic rating scales

This is one of the oldest and most popular appraisal methods. The rating scale is a list which consists of a number of performance factors, like quality and quantity of work, knowledge and skill levels, interpersonal relations, attendance, honesty and initiative. An immediate supervisor of a worker then rates the worker in each factor on a five-point scale.

Behaviourally anchored rating scales (BARS)

In this method, several important dimensions of a job are identified and defined. These dimensions include planning, communication or meeting deadlines. The identified dimensions are then described along a continuum scale from effective to ineffective behaviour. The worker is then rated accordingly on this scale against each dimension.

Multiple-person comparison

In this method an employee's performance is appraised against that of other workers. It is divided into group-ranking, individual ranking and paired comparison. In *group-ranking* the supervisor places employees into such groupings as the top 5 per cent, top 10 per cent, and so forth. In the *individual ranking* the workers are ranked from the best performer to the worst performer. In *paired comparison* a worker is compared with other employees in terms of his or her strengths and weaknesses. After all the paired-ratings have been done then an overall ranking of each employee is done.

Promotions, Transfers and Separations

Promotions

A promotion refers to the advancement of a worker to a better job in terms of more skill, responsibilities, status and remuneration. Promotions should be used by the educational management to place the most competent and productive worker on each job. It is an important reward to those employees who make the fullest use of their skills in productivity.

A well designed promotion policy must ensure that:

(i) There is a well established hierarchy of promotion grades for employees. The scheme for promotion from one grade to the next one should be clearly stipulated and objectively followed.

(ii) There is a clear statement by the educational management that promotions will, as much as possible, be filled from internal rather than external sources.

(iii) There is well established on-the-job and off-the job training programmes aimed at providing employees with the skills necessary for their promotion.

(iv) All vacancies for promotion are advertised for all concerned employees in advance.

(v) Employees who want to leave for greener pastures elsewhere are permitted to do so, because trying to hold them back against their wishes and without other better avenues may simply help in increasing the list of dissatisfied workers.

Transfers

A transfer is a useful technique for placing workers in places or positions where their maximum potentials can be utilised by the organisation. It helps in improving motivation and job satisfaction. Transfers can be on promotion, replacement or for convenience. There should be a clearly stated transfer policy which spells out the conditions and circumstances for transfer.

Separations

Separation is the process whereby a worker exits from his or her assigned job. This could be due to a number of reasons. These include: new career opportunities outside the organisation, dismissal, retirement or death. Educational management should have clearly stated policies on each kind of separation. A well documented terms of service programme must stipulate policies on all kinds of separation.

Educational Marketing

Educational marketing is an educational management's conscious effort to make an educational organisation attractive to the public through efficient and effective attainment of the educational objectives. Marketing is an important function of educational management, which is concerned with ensuring that what is happening within the precincts of an educational organisation is of great value to the society at large. A fundamental function of educational management is to ascertain that the educational objectives are achieved through a well planned acquisition of knowledge, skills and attitudes by the learners.

An educational organisation's market refers to a group of existing potential buyers and users of the goods and services offered by the educational organisation. It is a prime function of educational organisations to enable the educational system to achieve both the national and international educational objectives. These objectives are achieved through the acquisition of relevant knowledge, skills and attitudes.

The measurement of the production function of education is a very complex process. However, surrogate measurement techniques such as performance in examinations, can be used. The members of public and private organisations who are the potential buyers and users of the services offered by an educational organisation are concerned about how well students perform in the examinations in their school, college or university and also how adaptable the students are in the society on completion of their education. The society thus measures the productivity of an educational organisation in terms of success in examinations and societal adaptability.

Marketing an educational organisation, therefore, entails a concerted effort by the educational management to convince the public that the organisation is achieving the educational objectives, through its products, with efficiency and effectiveness. It is the quality of the product of an educational organisation which is instrumental in the promotion process. The quality of the students helps in creating a positive public behaviour towards the educational organisation. It is emphasised here that the promotion of the products of an educational organisation, in educational marketing, is an overt process which is mainly achieved through the quality of students completing their education in the organisation.

An educational organisation can only achieve its marketing strategies if it has the employees with both the quality and drive to help in steering it effectively towards its objectives. What an effective educational management does during the recruitment of employees is to use its marketing strategies to attract the best applicants, select them, train and develop then, and above all provide an enabling environment for their motivation and job satisfaction.

Summary

This Chapter begins by providing a basic concept on human resource development in educational management. The Chapter then proceeds to discuss the three basic human resources in an educational organisations namely: the teachers, the non-teaching staff and the students. This is followed by career development and Schein's career anchors. The four main stages in career development of a worker are also been discussed here.

The next part of the Chapter looks at job analysis, job description and job specification. This is followed by a discussion on recruitment, selection and placement. It is argued here that the recruitment of teachers to fill certain teaching positions must be preceded by their professional recruitment. Various selection methods are discussed here.

The last part of the Chapter dealt with training, development, performance appraisal, promotions, transfers, separations and educational marketing. This Chapter looks at educational management as a total function, that is to say it is a comprehensive management effort.

END NOTES

[1] D. Hall, *Careers in Organisations.* Glenview, Ill.: Scott, Foresman, 1976, p.4.

[2] E.A. Schein, *Career Dynamics,* Reading, Mass: Addison-Wesley, 1978, pp. 124-160.

[3] S.P. Robbins, *Organisational Behaviour: Concepts, Controversies and Applications.* New Jersey, Englewood Cliffs: Prentice Hall, 1989, p. 430.

[4] P. Pigors, and C.A. Myers. *Personnel Administration: A Point of View and a Method,* 7th. Ed. New York: McGraw-Hill Book Co., 1973, p. 248.

[5] K.J. Pratt, and S.G. Bennett. *Elements of Personnel Management,* 2nd Ed. London: Van Nostrand Reinhold Co. Ltd., 1989, pp. 131-132.

[6] R.D. Arvey, and J.E. Campion. "The employment interview: A summary and review of recent research", in *Personnel Psychology,* Summer 1982, 281-322.

Index

achievement motivation, 55
    see also need for achievement
achievement tests, 250
achievement-oriented leadership, 94
acognitive theories
    see content theories
Adams, Stacy, 63
adhocracy, 26
administration
    definition, 2
    practice, 3
    see also management
Administration Industrielle et Generale, 22
administrative inspection, 173
administrative man model, 151
    see also bounded theory rationality model
Alderfer, Clayton P., 52
all-channel (communication) network, 139
apprenticeship, 254
aptitude tests, 250
auditing, 228
    accounting and, 229
    external, 229
    objectives of, 228
    procedures, 230
authoritarian leadership
    see leadership
authority, 86, 99, 110
    definition, 99
    legal, 101
    types, 27, 101
    also formal authority
autocratic leadership, 87
balance sheet, 223
bank reconciliation, 224
Barnard, Chester, 4
behavioural science movement, 36
Bethlehem Steel Company, 19, 25
Bhagat, 73

book-keeping, 213
bounded rationality (decisioin making) model, 151
brainstorming, 166
Brech, E.F.L., 1
budget
    administration of, 211
    appraisal of, 212
budget plans, 201
budgetary process, 206, 212
    see budgetary process
budgeting, 24, 197, 205
    planning, 205
    principles of, 200
    programming, 205
    purpose, 198
    tentative budget, 209
    process
        see budgetary process
Bureau of Business Research, 88
bureaucracy, 26
bureaucratic organisation, 26
career anchors, 239
career development, 238
    stages in, 239
career, 238
cash book, 214
cash reconcilliation, 224
chain (communication) network, 138
Chassie, 73
circle (communication) network, 139
classical decision making
    see econologic decision making
classical management
    see scientific management
clearance account, 226
co-operative group effort, 174
co-ordinating, 24
coaching
    see mentoring
cognitive resonance theory
    see equity theory
Cohen, M.D., 8

commitment register (vote book), 218
communication, 127
    barriers
        distortion, 141
        filtering, 142
        language, 143
        omission, 142
        timeliness, 142
    definition, 127
    downward, 134
    networks, 137
        all channel, 139
        chain, 138
        circle, 139
        non-verbal, 132
        oral, 132
        upward, 135
        wheel, 138
        written, 132
        Y, 138
Conger, J.A., 97
consultative leadership
    see democratic leadership
content theories, 43
contingency theory, 89, 91
corrective feedback, 131
cost-benefit analysis, 197
Davis, K., 73
decision making,
    and problem-solving, 161
    definition, 145
    improvement, 166
    individual, 149
    models, 149
    non-programmed, 146
    normative model, 155
    participatory, 153
    styles, 156
    techniques 166
decisions
    programmed, 146
    types of, 146
Delphi technique, 168
democratic leadership
    see leadership
development

meaning, 251
directing, 24
disciplinary process, 121
discipline, 117
    corrective, 116
    meaning, 115
    preventive, 116
    principles of, 119
    progressive, 117
    types of, 116
    views of, 117
double entry book-keeping, 220
Drucker, Peter, 68
dual factor theory,
    see two-factor theory
Early Michigan Leadership Studies, 89
econologic (decisioin making) model, 149
economic man model, 149
    see also econologic model
education
    benefits, 196
    cost-benefit analysis in, 197
educational administration
    definition, 4
    see also educational management
educational management, 4
    and educational administration, 3
    and educational marketing, 260
    communication in, 128
    definition, 3, 4
    financial management, 196
    functions of, 11
    goal setting theory in, 69
    human resource in, 235
    perspective, 1
    scientific management in, 27
    training and, 252
educational marketing, 259
educational organisation, 4
    decisions in, 146
    discipline in, 115
    efficiency, 11

human resources, 235
   politics in, 108
   technology functions, 6
effective communication, 127
   barriers, 141
efficiency orientation, 174
Elmwood High, 162
employment tests, 249
environmental scanning, 147
equity theory, 63
ERG theory, 52
Erlandson, D.A., 74
Etzioni, A., 4
Evans, Martin, 93
existence needs, 52
expectancy theory, 58
expectancy, 60
Fayol's Bridge, 136
Fayol, Henri, 1, 2, 22, 23, 25, 136
Festinger, L., 63
Fiedler, Fred, 91
financial management, 196
financial accounting, 213
   books of accounts, 214
Follet, Mary Parker, 31
formal authority
   see authority
French, John, 102
Gantt Charts, 25
Gantt, 25
general supervision, 176
Gilbreth, Frank, 24
Gilbreth, Lilian, 24
goal setting theory, 66
Goldhammer, R., 176
Graen, George, 95
grapevine, 140
Great man theory, 89
Gregg, R.T., 180
group exchange theory, 89, 95
group ranking, 257
groupshift, 161

groupthink, 159
growth needs, 53
Gullick, Luther, 23, 24
Hackman, J. Richard, 70, 71, 72
Hamner, W.C., 64
Hamstra, B.W., 64
Hanson, E.M., 25
Harnett, D.R., 64
Hawthorne effect, 32, 37
Hawthorne studies, 31, 34, 36, 37
Herrick, N.Q., 75, 77
Herzberg's two-factor theory
   see two-factor theory
Herzberg, Fredrick, 51, 74, 77
heuristic, 151
horizontal communication, 136
hot stove rule, 119
House, Robert, 93, 97
human relations movement, 30, 88
human resource development, 235
ideal budget plan, 203
ideographic leadership, 98
Ilgen, D.R., 64
impersonal account records, 216
income generating account, 227
individual ranking, 257
induction, 251
   see also placement
influencing, 180
informational feedback, 131
initiation, 251
   see also placement
inspection, 192
inspector, 174
institutionalised power, 58
instructional supervision, 176, 185
   process, 185
instructional supervisor, 185
instrumentality, 60
intelligence tests, 249
internal auditing, 229
interpersonal communication, 129

    factors in, 133
    model, 129
    types of, 132
interview, 247
inventory, 219
Iowa leadership studies, 87
Janis, Irving, 159
job analysis, 241
    functions, 243
job characteristics model, 70
job description, 241, 242
Job diagnostic survey (JDS), 73
job rotation, 254
job satisfaction, 40
    contigency approach, 74
    definition, 41
    historical background, 42
    theories of, 40
    see also motivation
job satisfiers, 50
job specification, 241, 242
journal, 216
Kahn, R., 86
Kanungo, R.N., 97
Katz, D., 86
Katz, R., 73
Kiggundu, 73
King, N., 51
Koontz, 1
lateral communication
    see horizontal communication
Latham, Gary P., 66
leader behaviour description questionnaire (LBDQ), 88
leader member exchange (LMX), 95
leadership training, 99
leadership, 86, 110
    autocratic, 87
    charismatic, 96
    definition, 86
    democratic, 87, 98
    ideographic, 98
    laissez faire, 87

nomothetic, 98
  participative, 94
  studies, 87
  styles, 97
  supportive, 94
  theories, 89
  transactional, 98
least preferred co-worker (LPC) scale, 92
ledger, 216
Lewin, Kurt, 87
Locke, Edwin A., 66
Lwein, Kurt, 58
management by objectives (MBO), 68
management,
  definition, 1
  development of, 17
  practice, 3
  principles of 22
  scientific management, 19
  see also scientific management
March, J.G., 8
Maslow, 46, 49
Mayo, Professor Elton, 32
McClelland, David C., 55, 57
McGill University 97
McGregor, Douglas, 117, 119
mechanistic structure, 26
mentoring, 254
Midvale Steel Company, 19
Midwest Administrative Center, 98
Miller, 73
Miskel, C.G., 65
motivating potential score (MPS), 72
motivation, 40
  content theories, 43
  drives, 41
  historical background, 42
  integrated model, 78
  meaning, 40
  needs, 40
  theories of, 40, 43
need

    achievement, 55
    affiliation, 57
    power, 57
needs satisfaction questionnaire (NSQ), 47
needs-hierarchy theory, 44
nominal group techniquer (NGT), 167
non-teaching staff, 236
non-verbal communication, 132
    see also communication
O'Donnell, 1
Ohio State University, 88, 89
Okumbe, J.A., 77
Oldham, Greg, 70, 71, 72, 73
organic structure
    see adhocracy
organisation
    definition, 4
    goals, 5
organisational communication, 134, 140
organisational effectiveness, 9
organisational efficiency, 10
organising, 23
orientation, 251
    see also placement
Ortloff, W.G., 65
Owen, Robert, 43
paired comparison, 257
participative leadership
    see leadership
participatory (group) decisioin making, 153
Pastor, M.C., 74
path-goal theory, 89, 93
payment voucher, 220
performance appraisal, 251
    functions, 256
    meaning, 255
    methods, 256
performance simulation tests, 250
person specification
    see job specification
personal account records, 216
personality tests, 250

placement, 244, 251
planning, 23
planning, programming and budgeting systems (PPBS), 203, 204
Porter, L.W., 48, 52, 74
power, 86, 110
    and educational management, 106
    and politics, 108
    classification of, 102
    coersive, 104
    contigency model, 105
    definition, 102
    expert, 105
    legitimate, 104
    referent, 105
    reward, 102
problem-solving, 161, 162
process theories, 58
promotion, 258
Prudential Insurance Company, 89
rational decision making
    see econologic decision making
Raven, Bertran, 102
receipt books, 217
recruitment, 244
reinforcing feedback, 131
relatedness needs, 52
reporting, 24
retrospective decision model, 153
right of appeal, 121
Robbins, S.P., 80, 102
Roethlisberger, Professor Fritz, 33
role-playing, 255
Ronald, Lippitt, 87
satisficing, concept of, 152
Schein, E.A., 239
school as an industry, 10
school, economic function, 10
scientific management movement, 88
scientific management, 19, 27
    criticism, 29
    principles of, 20-21
selection, 244, 247

selective perception, 142
sensitivity training, 255
separation, 258, 259
Sergiovanni, T.J., 48
Sheppard, H.L., 75, 77
Shetty, Y.R., 105
silent language
    see non-verbal communication
Simon, Herbert, 99, 151, 169
simulations, 255
social exchange theory
    see equity theory
staffing, 23
Steers, R.M., 52, 74
Stogdill, Ralph, 90
stores ledger, 218
students, 237
supervision, 173
    activities, 178
    and inspection, 192
    clinical, 176
    definition, 175
    historical perspective, 173
    skills in, 182
Survey Research Center, 89
suspense account, 226
system analysis, 205
Taylor, Frederick, 19, 21, 23, 25, 34, 66
teaching practice, 185
Terburg, 73
theory of social and economic organisation, 25
theory X, 54, 117
theory Y, 54, 118
therbligs, 24
time-and-motion-studies, 21
Tolman, Edward, 58
traditional budget plan, 201
training, 251
    and development, 251
    functions, 253
    meaning, 251
    methods, 254

off-the-job, 259
on-the-job, 258
trait theory, 89
transfer, 258, 259
trial balance, 222
Trusty, F.M., 48
two-factor theory, 49
understudy, 255
University of Chicago, 98
University of Iowa, 87, 89, 97
University of Michigan, 89
Ure, Andrew, 43
Urwick, Lyndall, 23, 24
valence, 59
vertical dyad linkage (VDL) model, 95
vestibule training, 255
virement, 212
Vosecky, E.W., 200
vote-book register
  see commitment register
Vroom, Victor, 58, 155
Vroom-Yetton model, 155
Weber, Max, 25, 37, 102
Weberian bureaucracy, 27
Western Electric Company, 32
wheel (communication) network, 138
White, Ralph K., 87
work
  functions, 18
  meaning, 17
work plans, 211
"Y" (communication) network, 138
Yetton, Philip, 155

www.ingramcontent.com/pod-product-compliance
Lightning Source LLC
Chambersburg PA
CBHW061435300426
44114CB00014B/1698